CONTENTS

JULIUS CAESAR

William Shakespeare

SPARK PUBLISHING

SPARKNOTES is a registered trademark of SparkNotes LLC

Spark Publishing
A Division of Barnes & Noble
120 Fifth Avenue
New York, NY 10011
www.sparknotes.com

ISBN-13: 978-1-4114-0326-0
ISBN-10: 1-4114-0326-6

Please submit changes or report errors to www.sparknotes.com/errors.

Printed in the United States.

10 9 8 7 6 5 4 3 2 1

CONTEXT

LIKELY THE MOST INFLUENTIAL WRITER in all of English literature and certainly the most important playwright of the English Renaissance, William Shakespeare was born in 1564 in the town of Stratford-upon-Avon in Warwickshire, England. The son of a successful middle-class glove-maker, Shakespeare attended grammar school, but his formal education proceeded no further. In 1582, he married an older woman, Anne Hathaway, and had three children with her. Around 1590, he left his family behind and traveled to London to work as an actor and playwright. Public and critical acclaim quickly followed, and Shakespeare eventually became the most popular playwright in England and part owner of the Globe Theater. His career bridged the reigns of Elizabeth I (ruled 1558–1603) and James I (ruled 1603–1625); he was a favorite of both monarchs. Indeed, King James paid Shakespeare's theater company the greatest possible compliment by endowing its members with the status of king's players. Wealthy and renowned, Shakespeare retired to Stratford, and died in 1616 at the age of fifty-two. At the time of Shakespeare's death, such luminaries as Ben Jonson hailed him as the apogee of Renaissance theater.

Shakespeare's works were collected and printed in various editions in the century following his death, and by the early eighteenth century his reputation as the greatest poet ever to write in English was well established. The unprecedented admiration garnered by his works led to a fierce curiosity about Shakespeare's life, but the dearth of biographical information has left many details of Shakespeare's personal history shrouded in mystery. Some scholars have concluded from this lack and from Shakespeare's modest education that his plays were actually written by someone else—Francis Bacon and the Earl of Oxford are the two most popular candidates. The evidence for this claim, however, is overwhelmingly circumstantial, and few take the theory very seriously.

In the absence of definitive proof to the contrary, Shakespeare must be viewed as the author of the thirty-seven plays and 154 sonnets that bear his name. The legacy of this body of work is immense. A number of Shakespeare's plays seem to have transcended even

CONTEXT

the category of brilliance, becoming so influential as to affect profoundly the course of Western literature and culture ever after.

Julius Caesar takes place in ancient Rome in 44 B.C., when Rome was the center of an empire stretching from Britain to North Africa and from Persia to Spain. Yet even as the empire grew stronger, so, too, did the force of the dangers threatening its existence: Rome suffered from constant infighting between ambitious military leaders and the far weaker senators to whom they supposedly owed allegiance. The empire also suffered from a sharp division between citizens, who were represented in the senate, and the increasingly underrepresented plebeian masses. A succession of men aspired to become the absolute ruler of Rome, but only Julius Caesar seemed likely to achieve this status. Those citizens who favored more democratic rule feared that Caesar's power would lead to the enslavement of Roman citizens by one of their own. Therefore, a group of conspirators came together and assassinated Caesar. The assassination, however, failed to put an end to the power struggles dividing the empire, and civil war erupted shortly thereafter. The plot of Shakespeare's play includes the events leading up to the assassination of Caesar as well as much of the subsequent war, in which the deaths of the leading conspirators constituted a sort of revenge for the assassination.

Shakespeare's contemporaries, well versed in ancient Greek and Roman history, would very likely have detected parallels between *Julius Caesar*'s portrayal of the shift from republican to imperial Rome and the Elizabethan era's trend toward consolidated monarchal power. In 1599, when the play was first performed, Queen Elizabeth I had sat on the throne for nearly forty years, enlarging her power at the expense of the aristocracy and the House of Commons. As she was then sixty-six years old, her reign seemed likely to end soon, yet she lacked any heirs (as did Julius Caesar). Many feared that her death would plunge England into the kind of chaos that had plagued it during the fifteenth-century Wars of the Roses. In an age when censorship would have limited direct commentary on these worries, Shakespeare could nevertheless use the story of Caesar to comment on the political situation of his day.

As his chief source in writing *Julius Caesar,* Shakespeare probably used Thomas North's translation of Plutarch's *Lives of the Noble Greeks and Romans,* written in the first century A.D. Plutarch, who believed that history was propelled by the achievements of great men, saw the role of the biographer as inseparable from the role of the historian. Shakespeare followed Plutarch's lead by emphasizing how the actions of the leaders of Roman society, rather than class conflicts or larger political movements, determined history. However, while Shakespeare does focus on these key political figures, he does not ignore that their power rests, to some degree, on the fickle favor of the populace.

Contemporary accounts tell us that *Julius Caesar,* Shakespeare's shortest play, was first performed in 1599. It was probably the first play performed in the Globe Theater, the playhouse that was erected around that time in order to accommodate Shakespeare's increasingly successful theater company. However, the first authoritative text of the play did not appear until the 1623 First Folio edition. The elaborate stage directions suggest that this text was derived from the company's promptbook rather than Shakespeare's manuscript.

PLOT OVERVIEW

TWO TRIBUNES, FLAVIUS AND MURELLUS, find scores of Roman citizens wandering the streets, neglecting their work in order to watch Julius Caesar's triumphal parade: Caesar has defeated the sons of the deceased Roman general Pompey, his archrival, in battle. The tribunes scold the citizens for abandoning their duties and remove decorations from Caesar's statues. Caesar enters with his entourage, including the military and political figures Brutus, Cassius, and Antony. A Soothsayer calls out to Caesar to "beware the Ides of March," but Caesar ignores him and proceeds with his victory celebration (I.ii.19, I.ii.25).

Cassius and Brutus, both longtime intimates of Caesar and each other, converse. Cassius tells Brutus that he has seemed distant lately; Brutus replies that he has been at war with himself. Cassius states that he wishes Brutus could see himself as others see him, for then Brutus would realize how honored and respected he is. Brutus says that he fears that the people want Caesar to become king, which would overturn the republic. Cassius concurs that Caesar is treated like a god though he is merely a man, no better than Brutus or Cassius. Cassius recalls incidents of Caesar's physical weakness and marvels that this fallible man has become so powerful. He blames his and Brutus's lack of will for allowing Caesar's rise to power: surely the rise of such a man cannot be the work of fate. Brutus considers Cassius's words as Caesar returns. Upon seeing Cassius, Caesar tells Antony that he deeply distrusts Cassius.

Caesar departs, and another politician, Casca, tells Brutus and Cassius that, during the celebration, Antony offered the crown to Caesar three times and the people cheered, but Caesar refused it each time. He reports that Caesar then fell to the ground and had some kind of seizure before the crowd; his demonstration of weakness, however, did not alter the plebeians' devotion to him. Brutus goes home to consider Cassius's words regarding Caesar's poor qualifications to rule, while Cassius hatches a plot to draw Brutus into a conspiracy against Caesar.

That night, Rome is plagued with violent weather and a variety of bad omens and portents. Brutus finds letters in his house apparently written by Roman citizens worried that Caesar has become too powerful. The letters have in fact been forged and planted by Cassius, who knows that if Brutus believes it is the people's will, he will support a plot to remove Caesar from power. A committed supporter of the republic, Brutus fears the possibility of a dictator-led empire, worrying that the populace would lose its voice. Cassius arrives at Brutus's home with his conspirators, and Brutus, who has already been won over by the letters, takes control of the meeting. The men agree to lure Caesar from his house and kill him. Cassius wants to kill Antony too, for Antony will surely try to hinder their plans, but Brutus disagrees, believing that too many deaths will render their plot too bloody and dishonor them. Having agreed to spare Antony, the conspirators depart. Portia, Brutus's wife, observes that Brutus appears preoccupied. She pleads with him to confide in her, but he rebuffs her.

Caesar prepares to go to the Senate. His wife, Calpurnia, begs him not to go, describing recent nightmares she has had in which a statue of Caesar streamed with blood and smiling men bathed their hands in the blood. Caesar refuses to yield to fear and insists on going about his daily business. Finally, Calpurnia convinces him to stay home—if not out of caution, then as a favor to her. But Decius, one of the conspirators, then arrives and convinces Caesar that Calpurnia has misinterpreted her dreams and the recent omens. Caesar departs for the Senate in the company of the conspirators.

As Caesar proceeds through the streets toward the Senate, the Soothsayer again tries but fails to get his attention. The citizen Artemidorus hands him a letter warning him about the conspirators, but Caesar refuses to read it, saying that his closest personal concerns are his last priority. At the Senate, the conspirators speak to Caesar, bowing at his feet and encircling him. One by one, they stab him to death. When Caesar sees his dear friend Brutus among his murderers, he gives up his struggle and dies.

The murderers bathe their hands and swords in Caesar's blood, thus bringing Calpurnia's premonition to fruition. Antony, having been led away on a false pretext, returns and pledges allegiance to Brutus but weeps over Caesar's body. He shakes hands with the conspirators, thus marking them all as guilty while appearing to make a gesture of conciliation. When Antony asks why they killed Caesar, Brutus replies that he will explain their purpose in a funeral oration. Antony asks to be allowed to speak over the body as well; Brutus grants his permission, though Cassius remains suspicious of

Antony. The conspirators depart, and Antony, alone now, swears that Caesar's death shall be avenged.

Brutus and Cassius go to the Forum to speak to the public. Cassius exits to address another part of the crowd. Brutus declares to the masses that though he loved Caesar, he loves Rome more, and Caesar's ambition posed a danger to Roman liberty. The speech placates the crowd. Antony appears with Caesar's body, and Brutus departs after turning the pulpit over to Antony. Repeatedly referring to Brutus as "an honorable man," Antony's speech becomes increasingly sarcastic; questioning the claims that Brutus made in his speech that Caesar acted only out of ambition, Antony points out that Caesar brought much wealth and glory to Rome, and three times turned down offers of the crown. Antony then produces Caesar's will but announces that he will not read it, for it would upset the people inordinately. The crowd nevertheless begs him to read the will, so he descends from the pulpit to stand next to Caesar's body. He describes Caesar's horrible death and shows Caesar's wounded body to the crowd. He then reads Caesar's will, which bequeaths a sum of money to every citizen and orders that his private gardens be made public. The crowd becomes enraged that this generous man lies dead; calling Brutus and Cassius traitors, the masses set off to drive them from the city.

Meanwhile, Caesar's adopted son and appointed successor, Octavius, arrives in Rome and forms a three-person coalition with Antony and Lepidus. They prepare to fight Cassius and Brutus, who have been driven into exile and are raising armies outside the city. At the conspirators' camp, Brutus and Cassius have a heated argument regarding matters of money and honor, but they ultimately reconcile. Brutus reveals that he is sick with grief, for in his absence Portia has killed herself. The two continue to prepare for battle with Antony and Octavius. That night, the Ghost of Caesar appears to Brutus, announcing that Brutus will meet him again on the battlefield.

Octavius and Antony march their army toward Brutus and Cassius. Antony tells Octavius where to attack, but Octavius says that he will make his own orders; he is already asserting his authority as the heir of Caesar and the next ruler of Rome. The opposing generals meet on the battlefield and exchange insults before beginning combat.

Cassius witnesses his own men fleeing and hears that Brutus's men are not performing effectively. Cassius sends one of his men,

Pindarus, to see how matters are progressing. From afar, Pindarus sees one of their leaders, Cassius's best friend, Titinius, being surrounded by cheering troops and concludes that he has been captured. Cassius despairs and orders Pindarus to kill him with his own sword. He dies proclaiming that Caesar is avenged. Titinius himself then arrives—the men encircling him were actually his comrades, cheering a victory he had earned. Titinius sees Cassius's corpse and, mourning the death of his friend, kills himself.

Brutus learns of the deaths of Cassius and Titinius with a heavy heart, and prepares to take on the Romans again. When his army loses, doom appears imminent. Brutus asks one of his men to hold his sword while he impales himself on it. Finally, Caesar can rest satisfied, he says as he dies. Octavius and Antony arrive. Antony speaks over Brutus's body, calling him the noblest Roman of all. While the other conspirators acted out of envy and ambition, he observes, Brutus genuinely believed that he acted for the benefit of Rome. Octavius orders that Brutus be buried in the most honorable way. The men then depart to celebrate their victory.

CHARACTER LIST

Brutus   A supporter of the republic who believes strongly in a government guided by the votes of senators. While Brutus loves Caesar as a friend, he opposes the ascension of any single man to the position of dictator, and he fears that Caesar aspires to such power. Brutus's inflexible sense of honor makes it easy for Caesar's enemies to manipulate him into believing that Caesar must die in order to preserve the republic. While the other conspirators act out of envy and rivalry, only Brutus truly believes that Caesar's death will benefit Rome. Unlike Caesar, Brutus is able to separate completely his public life from his private life; by giving priority to matters of state, he epitomizes Roman virtue. Torn between his loyalty to Caesar and his allegiance to the state, Brutus becomes the tragic hero of the play.

Julius Caesar A great Roman general and senator, recently returned to Rome in triumph after a successful military campaign. While his good friend Brutus worries that Caesar may aspire to dictatorship over the Roman republic, Caesar seems to show no such inclination, declining the crown several times. Yet while Caesar may not be unduly power-hungry, he does possess his share of flaws. He is unable to separate his public life from his private life, and, seduced by the populace's increasing idealization and idolization of his image, he ignores ill omens and threats against his life, believing himself as eternal as the North Star.

Antony   A friend of Caesar. Antony claims allegiance to Brutus and the conspirators after Caesar's death in order to save his own life. Later, however, when speaking a funeral oration over Caesar's body, he spectacularly persuades the audience to withdraw its support of Brutus and instead condemn him as a traitor. With tears on his cheeks and Caesar's will in his hand,

Antony engages masterful rhetoric to stir the crowd to revolt against the conspirators. Antony's desire to exclude Lepidus from the power that Antony and Octavius intend to share hints at his own ambitious nature.

Cassius   A talented general and longtime acquaintance of Caesar. Cassius dislikes the fact that Caesar has become godlike in the eyes of the Romans. He slyly leads Brutus to believe that Caesar has become too powerful and must die, finally converting Brutus to his cause by sending him forged letters claiming that the Roman people support the death of Caesar. Impulsive and unscrupulous, Cassius harbors no illusions about the way the political world works. A shrewd opportunist, he proves successful but lacks integrity.

Octavius   Caesar's adopted son and appointed successor. Octavius, who had been traveling abroad, returns after Caesar's death; he then joins with Antony and sets off to fight Cassius and Brutus. Antony tries to control Octavius's movements, but Octavius follows his adopted father's example and emerges as the authoritative figure, paving the way for his eventual seizure of the reins of Roman government.

Casca   A public figure opposed to Caesar's rise to power. Casca relates to Cassius and Brutus how Antony offered the crown to Caesar three times and how each time Caesar declined it. He believes, however, that Caesar is the consummate actor, lulling the populace into believing that he has no personal ambition.

Calpurnia   Caesar's wife. Calpurnia invests great authority in omens and portents. She warns Caesar against going to the Senate on the Ides of March, since she has had terrible nightmares and heard reports of many bad omens. Nevertheless, Caesar's ambition ultimately causes him to disregard her advice.

Portia   Brutus's wife; the daughter of a noble Roman who took sides against Caesar. Portia, accustomed to being Brutus's confidante, is upset to find him so reluctant to speak his mind when she finds him troubled. Brutus later hears that Portia has killed herself out of grief that Antony and Octavius have become so powerful.

Flavius   A tribune (an official elected by the people to protect their rights). Flavius condemns the plebeians for their fickleness in cheering Caesar, when once they cheered for Caesar's enemy Pompey. Flavius is punished along with Murellus for removing the decorations from Caesar's statues during Caesar's triumphal parade.

Cicero   A Roman senator renowned for his oratorical skill. Cicero speaks at Caesar's triumphal parade. He later dies at the order of Antony, Octavius, and Lepidus.

Lepidus   The third member of Antony and Octavius's coalition. Though Antony has a low opinion of Lepidus, Octavius trusts his loyalty.

Murellus   Like Flavius, a tribune who condemns the plebeians for their fickleness in cheering Caesar, when once they cheered for Caesar's enemy Pompey. Murellus and Flavius are punished for removing the decorations from Caesar's statues during Caesar's triumphal parade.

Decius   A member of the conspiracy. Decius convinces Caesar that Calpurnia misinterpreted her dire nightmares and that, in fact, no danger awaits him at the Senate. Decius leads Caesar right into the hands of the conspirators.

Analysis of Major Characters

Brutus

Brutus emerges as the most complex character in *Julius Caesar* and is also the play's tragic hero. In his soliloquies, the audience gains insight into the complexities of his motives. He is a powerful public figure, but he appears also as a husband, a master to his servants, a dignified military leader, and a loving friend. The conflicting value systems that battle with each other in the play as a whole are enacted on a microcosmic level in Brutus's mind. Even after Brutus has committed the assassination with the other members of the conspiracy, questions remain as to whether, in light of his friendship with Caesar, the murder was a noble, decidedly selfless act or proof of a truly evil callousness, a gross indifference to the ties of friendship and a failure to be moved by the power of a truly great man.

Brutus's rigid idealism is both his greatest virtue and his most deadly flaw. In the world of the play, where self-serving ambition seems to dominate all other motivations, Brutus lives up to Antony's elegiac description of him as "the noblest of Romans." However, his commitment to principle repeatedly leads him to make miscalculations: wanting to curtail violence, he ignores Cassius's suggestion that the conspirators kill Antony as well as Caesar. In another moment of naïve idealism, he again ignores Cassius's advice and allows Antony to speak a funeral oration over Caesar's body. As a result, Brutus forfeits the authority of having the last word on the murder and thus allows Antony to incite the plebeians to riot against him and the other conspirators. Brutus later endangers his good relationship with Cassius by self-righteously condemning what he sees as dishonorable fund-raising tactics on Cassius's part. In all of these episodes, Brutus acts out of a desire to limit the self-serving aspects of his actions; ironically, however, in each incident he dooms the very cause that he seeks to promote, thus serving no one at all.

Julius Caesar

The conspirators charge Caesar with ambition, and his behavior substantiates this judgment: he does vie for absolute power over Rome, reveling in the homage he receives from others and in his conception of himself as a figure who will live on forever in men's minds. However, his faith in his own permanence—in the sense of both his loyalty to principles and his fixture as a public institution—eventually proves his undoing. At first, he stubbornly refuses to heed the nightmares of his wife, Calpurnia, and the supernatural omens pervading the atmosphere. Though he is eventually persuaded not to go to the Senate, Caesar ultimately lets his ambition get the better of him, as the prospect of being crowned king proves too glorious to resist.

Caesar's conflation of his public image with his private self helps bring about his death, since he mistakenly believes that the immortal status granted to his public self somehow protects his mortal body. Still, in many ways, Caesar's faith that he is eternal proves valid by the end of the play: by Act V, scene iii, Brutus is attributing his and Cassius's misfortunes to Caesar's power reaching from beyond the grave. Caesar's aura seems to affect the general outcome of events in a mystic manner, while also inspiring Octavius and Antony and strengthening their determination. As Octavius ultimately assumes the title Caesar, Caesar's permanence is indeed established in some respect.

Antony

Antony proves strong in all of the ways that Brutus proves weak. His impulsive, improvisatory nature serves him perfectly, first to persuade the conspirators that he is on their side, thus gaining their leniency, and then to persuade the plebeians of the conspirators' injustice, thus gaining the masses' political support. Not too scrupulous to stoop to deceit and duplicity, as Brutus claims to be, Antony proves himself a consummate politician, using gestures and skilled rhetoric to his advantage. He responds to subtle cues among both his nemeses and his allies to know exactly how he must conduct himself at each particular moment in order to gain the most advantage. In both his eulogy for Caesar and the play as a whole, Antony is adept at tailoring his words and actions to his audiences' desires. Unlike Brutus, who prides himself on acting solely with respect to virtue and blinding himself to his personal concerns, Antony never separates his private affairs from his public actions.

THEMES, MOTIFS & SYMBOLS

THEMES

Themes are the fundamental and often universal ideas explored in a literary work.

FATE VERSUS FREE WILL

Julius Caesar raises many questions about the force of fate in life versus the capacity for free will. Cassius refuses to accept Caesar's rising power and deems a belief in fate to be nothing more than a form of passivity or cowardice. He says to Brutus: "Men at some-time were masters of their fates. / The fault, dear Brutus, is not in our stars, / But in ourselves, that we are underlings" (I.ii.140–142). Cassius urges a return to a more noble, self-possessed attitude toward life, blaming his and Brutus's submissive stance not on a pre-destined plan but on their failure to assert themselves.

Ultimately, the play seems to support a philosophy in which fate and freedom maintain a delicate coexistence. Thus Caesar declares: "It seems to me most strange that men should fear, / Seeing that death, a necessary end, / Will come when it will come" (II.ii.35–37). In other words, Caesar recognizes that certain events lie beyond human control; to crouch in fear of them is to enter a paralysis equal to, if not worse than, death. It is to surrender any capacity for freedom and agency that one might actually possess. Indeed, perhaps to face death head-on, to die bravely and honorably, is Caesar's best course: in the end, Brutus interprets his and Cassius's defeat as the work of Caesar's ghost—not just his apparition, but also the force of the people's devotion to him, the strong legacy of a man who refused any fear of fate and, in his disregard of fate, seems to have transcended it.

PUBLIC SELF VERSUS PRIVATE SELF

Much of the play's tragedy stems from the characters' neglect of private feelings and loyalties in favor of what they believe to be the public good. Similarly, characters confuse their private selves with their public selves, hardening and dehumanizing themselves or transforming themselves into ruthless political machines. Brutus

15

rebuffs his wife, Portia, when she pleads with him to confide in her; believing himself to be acting on the people's will, he forges ahead with the murder of Caesar, despite their close friendship. Brutus puts aside his personal loyalties and shuns thoughts of Caesar the man, his friend; instead, he acts on what he believes to be the public's wishes and kills Caesar the leader, the imminent dictator. Cassius can be seen as a man who has gone to the extreme in cultivating his public persona. Caesar, describing his distrust of Cassius, tells Antony that the problem with Cassius is his lack of a private life—his seeming refusal to acknowledge his own sensibilities or to nurture his own spirit. Such a man, Caesar fears, will let nothing interfere with his ambition. Indeed, Cassius lacks all sense of personal honor and shows himself to be a ruthless schemer.

Ultimately, neglecting private sentiments to follow public concerns brings Caesar to his death. Although Caesar does briefly agree to stay home from the Senate in order to please Calpurnia, who has dreamed of his murder, he gives way to ambition when Decius tells him that the senators plan to offer him the crown. Caesar's public self again takes precedence. Tragically, he no longer sees the difference between his omnipotent, immortal public image and his vulnerable human body. Just preceding his death, Caesar refuses Artemidorus's pleas to speak with him, saying that he gives last priority to his most personal concerns. He thus endangers himself by believing that the strength of his public self will protect his private self.

MISINTERPRETATIONS AND MISREADINGS

Much of the play deals with the characters' failures to interpret correctly the omens that they encounter. As Cicero says, "Men may construe things after their fashion, / Clean from the purpose of the things themselves" (I.iii.34–35). Thus, the night preceding Caesar's appearance at the Senate is full of portents, but no one reads them accurately: Cassius takes them to signify the danger that Caesar's impending coronation would bring to the state, when, if anything, they warn of the destruction that Cassius himself threatens. There are calculated misreadings as well: Cassius manipulates Brutus into joining the conspiracy by means of forged letters, knowing that Brutus's trusting nature will cause him to accept the letters as authentic pleas from the Roman people.

The circumstances of Cassius's death represent another instance of misinterpretation. Pindarus's erroneous conclusion that Titinius has been captured by the enemy, when in fact Titinius has reunited with friendly forces, is the piece of misinformation that prompts Cassius to seek death. Thus, in the world of politics portrayed in *Julius Caesar,* the inability to read people and events leads to downfall; conversely, the ability to do so is the key to survival. With so much ambition and rivalry, the ability to gauge the public's opinion as well as the resentment or loyalty of one's fellow politicians can guide one to success. Antony proves masterful at recognizing his situation, and his accurate reading of the crowd's emotions during his funeral oration for Caesar allows him to win the masses over to his side.

INFLEXIBILITY VERSUS COMPROMISE

Both Brutus and Caesar are stubborn, rather inflexible people who ultimately suffer fatally for it. In the play's aggressive political landscape, individuals succeed through adaptability, bargaining, and compromise. Brutus's rigid though honorable ideals leave him open for manipulation by Cassius. He believes so thoroughly in the purpose of the assassination that he does not perceive the need for excessive political maneuvering to justify the murder. Equally resolute, Caesar prides himself on his steadfastness; yet this constancy helps bring about his death, as he refuses to heed ill omens and goes willingly to the Senate, into the hands of his murderers.

Antony proves perhaps the most adaptable of all of the politicians: while his speech to the Roman citizens centers on Caesar's generosity toward each citizen, he later searches for ways to turn these funds into cash in order to raise an army against Brutus and Cassius. Although he gains power by offering to honor Caesar's will and provide the citizens their rightful money, it becomes clear that ethical concerns will not prevent him from using the funds in a more politically expedient manner. Antony is a successful politician—yet the question of morality remains. There seems to be no way to reconcile firm moral principles with success in politics in Shakespeare's rendition of ancient Rome; thus each character struggles toward a different solution.

RHETORIC AND POWER

Julius Caesar gives detailed consideration to the relationship between rhetoric and power. The ability to make things happen by words alone is the most powerful type of authority. Early in the play, it is established that Caesar has this type of absolute authority: "When Caesar says 'Do this,' it is performed," says Antony, who attaches a similar weight to Octavius's words toward the end of the play (I.ii.12). Words also serve to move hearts and minds, as Act III

THEMES

evidences. Antony cleverly convinces the conspirators of his desire to side with them: "Let each man render me with his bloody hand" (III.i.185). Under the guise of a gesture of friendship, Antony actually marks the conspirators for vengeance. In the Forum, Brutus speaks to the crowd and appeals to its love of liberty in order to justify the killing of Caesar. He also makes ample reference to the honor in which he is generally esteemed so as to validate further his explanation of the deed. Antony likewise wins the crowd's favor, using persuasive rhetoric to whip the masses into a frenzy so great that they don't even realize the fickleness of their favor.

MOTIFS

Motifs are recurring structures, contrasts, and literary devices that can help to develop and inform the text's major themes.

OMENS AND PORTENTS

Throughout the play, omens and portents manifest themselves, each serving to crystallize the larger themes of fate and misinterpretation of signs. Until Caesar's death, each time an omen or nightmare is reported, the audience is reminded of Caesar's impending demise. The audience wonders whether these portents simply announce what is fated to occur or whether they serve as warnings for what might occur if the characters do not take active steps to change their behavior. Whether or not individuals can affect their destinies, characters repeatedly fail to interpret the omens correctly. In a larger sense, the omens in *Julius Caesar* thus imply the dangers of failing to perceive and analyze the details of one's world.

LETTERS

The motif of letters represents an interesting counterpart to the force of oral rhetoric in the play. Oral rhetoric depends upon a direct, dialogic interaction between speaker and audience: depending on how the listeners respond to a certain statement, the orator can alter his or her speech and intonations accordingly. In contrast, the power of a written letter depends more fully on the addressee; whereas an orator must read the emotions of the crowd, the act of reading is undertaken solely by the recipient of the letter. Thus, when Brutus receives the forged letter from Cassius in Act II, scene i, the letter has an effect because Brutus allows it to do so; it is he who grants it its full power. In contrast, Caesar refuses to read the letter that Artemidorus tries to hand him in Act III, scene i, as he is heading to the Senate. Predisposed to ignore personal affairs, Caesar denies the letter any reading at all and thus negates the potential power of the words written inside.

Symbols

Symbols are objects, characters, figures, and colors used to represent abstract ideas or concepts.

Women and Wives

While one could try to analyze Calpurnia and Portia as full characters in their own right, they function primarily not as sympathetic personalities or sources of insight or poetry but rather as symbols for the private, domestic realm. Both women plead with their husbands to be more aware of their private needs and feelings (Portia in Act II, scene i; Calpurnia in Act III, scene ii). Caesar and Brutus rebuff the pleas of their respective wives, however; they not only prioritize public matters but also actively disregard their private emotions and intuitions. As such, Calpurnia and Portia are powerless figures, willing though unable to help and comfort Caesar and Brutus.

SUMMARY & ANALYSIS

ACT I, SCENE I

SUMMARY

Two tribunes, Flavius and Murellus, enter a Roman street, along with various commoners. Flavius and Murellus derisively order the commoners to return home and get back to work: "What, know you not, / Being mechanical, you ought not walk / Upon a labouring day without the sign / Of your profession?" (I.i.2–5). Murellus engages a cobbler in a lengthy inquiry about his profession; misinterpreting the cobbler's punning replies, Murellus quickly grows angry with him. Flavius interjects to ask why the cobbler is not in his shop working. The cobbler explains that he is taking a holiday from work in order to observe the triumph (a lavish parade celebrating military victory)—he wants to watch Caesar's procession through the city, which will include the captives won in a recent battle against his archrival Pompey.

Murellus scolds the cobbler and attempts to diminish the significance of Caesar's victory over Pompey and his consequent triumph. "What conquest brings he home? / What tributaries follow him [Caesar] to Rome / To grace in captive bonds his chariot wheels?" Murellus asks, suggesting that Caesar's victory does not merit a triumph since it involves no conquering of a foreign foe to the greater glory of Rome (I.i.31–33). Murellus reminds the commoners of the days when they used to gather to watch and cheer for Pompey's triumphant returns from battle. Now, however, due to a mere twist of fate, they rush out to celebrate his downfall. Murellus scolds them further for their disloyalty, ordering them to "pray to the gods to intermit the plague / That needs must light on this ingratitude" (I.i.53–54).

The commoners leave, and Flavius instructs Murellus to go to the Capitol, a hill on which rests a temple on whose altars victorious generals offer sacrifice, and remove any crowns placed on statues of Caesar. Flavius adds that he will thin the crowds of commoners observing the triumph and directs Murellus to do likewise, for if they can regulate Caesar's popular support, they will be able to regulate his power ("These growing feathers plucked from Caesar's wing / Will make him fly an ordinary pitch" [I.i.71–72]).

ANALYSIS

Although the play opens with Flavius and Murellus noting the fickle nature of the public's devotion—the crowd now celebrates Caesar's defeat of Pompey when once it celebrated Pompey's victories—loyalty to Caesar nonetheless appears to be growing with exceptional force. Caesar's power and influence are likewise strong: Flavius and Murellus are later punished for removing the decorations from Caesar's statues.

It is interesting to note the difference between the manner in which Flavius and Murellus conceive of the cobbler and that in which Shakespeare has created him. The cobbler is a typically Shakespearean character—a host of puns and bawdy references reveal his dexterity with language ("all that I live by is with the awl. I meddle / with no tradesman's matters, nor women's matters" [I.i.21–22]). The tribunes, however, preoccupied with class distinctions, view the cobbler as nothing more than a plebeian ruffian. Flavius's reproach of the cobbler for not having his tools about him on a workday reveals his belief that a laborer can be good for one thing and one thing only: laboring. Murellus similarly assumes that the cobbler is stupid, although, ironically, it is Murellus himself who misunderstands the cobbler's answers to his questions. Murellus is unwilling to interpret the cobbler's shift in allegiance from Pompey to Caesar as anything but a manifestation of dim-witted forgetfulness.

Flavius and Murellus's concern about Caesar's meteoric rise to power reflects English sentiment during the Elizabethan age about the consolidation of power in other parts of Europe. The strengthening of the absolutist monarchies in such sovereignties as France and Spain during the sixteenth century threatened the stability of the somewhat more balanced English political system, which, though it was hardly democratic in the modern sense of the word, at least provided nobles and elected representatives with some means of checking royal authority. Caesar's ascendance helped to effect Rome's transition from republic to empire, and Shakespeare's depiction of the prospect of Caesar's assumption of dictatorial power can be seen as a comment upon the gradual shift toward centralization of power that was taking place in Europe.

In addition, Shakespeare's illustration of the fickleness of the Roman public proves particularly relevant to the English political scene of the time. Queen Elizabeth I was nearing the end of her life but had neither produced nor named an heir. Anxiety mounted concerning who her successor would be. People feared that without resort to the established, accepted means of transferring power—passing it down the family line—England might plunge into the sort of chaotic power struggle that had plagued it in the fifteenth century, during the Wars of the Roses. Flavius and Murellus's interest in controlling the populace lays the groundwork for Brutus's and Antony's manipulations of public opinion after Caesar's death. Shakespeare thus makes it clear that the struggle for power will involve a battle among the leaders to win public favor with displays of bravery and convincing rhetoric. Considering political history in the centuries after Shakespeare wrote *Julius Caesar,* especially in the twentieth century, when Benito Mussolini and Adolf Hitler consolidated their respective regimes by whipping up in the masses the overzealous nationalism that had pervaded nineteenth-century Italy and Germany, the play is remarkably prescient.

ACT I, SCENE II

SUMMARY

Caesar enters a public square with Antony, Calpurnia, Portia, Decius, Cicero, Brutus, Cassius, Casca, and a Soothsayer; he is followed by a throng of citizens and then by Flavius and Murellus. Antony, dressed to celebrate the feast day, readies himself for a ceremonial run through the city. Caesar urges him to touch Calpurnia, Caesar's wife, as he runs, since Roman superstition holds that the touch of a ceremonial runner will cure barrenness. Antony agrees, declaring that whatever Caesar says is certain to become fact.

The Soothsayer calls out from the crowd to Caesar, telling him to beware the Ides of March. (The "ides" refers to the fifteenth day of March, May, July, and October and the thirteenth day of the other months in the ancient Roman calendar.) Caesar pauses and asks the man to come forward; the Soothsayer repeats himself. Caesar ultimately dismisses the warning, and the procession departs. Brutus and Cassius remain. Cassius asks Brutus why he has not seemed himself lately. Brutus replies that he has been quiet because he has been plagued with conflicting thoughts. But he assures Cassius that even though his mind is at war with itself, he will not let his inner turmoil affect his friendships.

Cassius and Brutus speak together. Cassius asks Brutus if Brutus can see his own face; Brutus replies that he cannot. Cassius then declares that Brutus is unable to see what everyone else does, namely, that Brutus is widely respected. Noting that no mirror could reveal

Brutus's worthiness to himself, Cassius offers to serve as a human mirror so that Brutus may discover himself and conceive of himself in new ways.

Brutus hears shouting and says that he fears that the people want to make Caesar their king. When Cassius asks, Brutus affirms that he would rather that Caesar not assume the position. Brutus adds that he loves Caesar but that he also loves honor, and that he loves honor even more than he fears death. Cassius replies that he, too, recoils at the thought of kneeling in awe before someone whom he does not consider his superior, and declares, "I was born as free as Caesar, so were you. / We both have fed as well, and we can both / Endure the winter's cold as well as he" (I.ii.99–101). Cassius recalls a windy day when he and Caesar stood on the banks of the Tiber River, and Caesar dared him to swim to a distant point. They raced through the water, but Caesar became weak and asked Cassius to save him. Cassius had to drag him from the water. Cassius also recounts an episode when Caesar had a fever in Spain and experienced a seizure. Cassius marvels to think that a man with such a feeble constitution should now stand at the head of the civilized world.

Caesar stands like a Colossus over the world, Cassius continues, while Cassius and Brutus creep about under his legs. He tells Brutus that they owe their underling status not to fate but to their own failure to take action. He questions the difference between the name "Caesar" and the name "Brutus": why should Caesar's name be more celebrated than Brutus's when, spoken together, the names sound equally pleasing and thus suggest that the men should hold equal power? He wonders in what sort of age they are living when one man can tower over the rest of the population. Brutus responds that he will consider Cassius's words. Although unwilling to be further persuaded, he admits that he would rather not be a citizen of Rome in such strange times as the present.

Meanwhile, Caesar and his train return. Caesar sees Cassius and comments to Antony that Cassius looks like a man who thinks too much; such men are dangerous, he adds. Antony tells Caesar not to worry, but Caesar replies that he prefers to avoid Cassius: Cassius reads too much and finds no enjoyment in plays or music—such men are never at ease while someone greater than themselves holds the reins of power. Caesar urges Antony to come to his right side—he is deaf in his left ear—and tell him what he thinks of Cassius. Shortly, Caesar and his train depart.

Brutus and Cassius take Casca aside to ask him what happened at the procession. Casca relates that Antony offered a crown to Caesar three times, but Caesar refused it each time. While the crowd cheered for him, Caesar fell to the ground in a fit. Brutus speculates that Caesar has "the falling sickness" (a term for epilepsy in Elizabethan times). Casca notes, however, that Caesar's fit did not seem to affect his authority: although he suffered his seizure directly before the crowd, the people did not cease to express their love. Casca adds that the great orator Cicero spoke in Greek, but that he couldn't understand him at all, saying "it was Greek to me" (I.ii.278). He concludes by reporting that Flavius and Murellus were deprived of their positions as civil servants for removing decorations from Caesar's statues. Casca then departs, followed by Brutus.

Cassius, alone now, says that while he believes that Brutus is noble, he hopes that Brutus's noble nature may yet be bent: "For who so firm that cannot be seduced?" he asks rhetorically (I.ii.306). He decides to forge letters from Roman citizens declaring their support for Brutus and their fear of Caesar's ascent to power; he will throw them into Brutus's house that evening.

ANALYSIS

While the opening scene illustrates Caesar's popularity with the masses, the audience's first direct encounter with him presents an omen of his imminent fall. Caesar's choice to ignore the Soothsayer's advice proves the first in a series of failures to heed warnings about his fate. Just as Caesar himself proves fallible, his power proves imperfect. When Caesar orders Antony to touch Calpurnia, Antony replies that Caesar need merely speak and his word will become fact—that is, Caesar's authority is so strong that his word immediately brings about the requested action. However, while the masses may conceive of Caesar's power thus, Caesar's order to Antony alerts us to the reality that he and his wife have been unable to produce a child. The implication that Caesar may be impotent or sterile is the first—and, for a potential monarch, the most damaging—of his physical shortcomings to be revealed in the play.

This conversation between Brutus and Cassius reveals the respective characters of the two men, who will emerge as the foremost conspirators against Caesar. Brutus appears to be a man at war with himself, torn between his love for Caesar and his honorable concern for Rome. He worries that it is not in Rome's best interest for Caesar to become king, yet he hates to oppose his friend. Cassius steps into Brutus's personal crisis and begins his campaign to turn Brutus against Caesar, flattering Brutus's pride by offering to be his mirror and thus relaying to him the ostensible high regard in which the citizens hold him.

Cassius compounds Brutus's alarm about Caesar's growing power with references to his weak physical state: he lacks stamina and is probably epileptic. But Cassius observes only Caesar's frail human body, his private self. When he urges Brutus to consider that the name of Brutus should be as powerful as the name of Caesar, he fails to understand that Caesar's real power is not affected by private infirmities but rather rests in his public persona, whose strength is derived from the goodwill and good opinion of the populace.

Caesar, on the other hand, shows much more perceptiveness in his analysis of Cassius; he observes both Cassius's private and public personas and notices a discord. He is made uneasy by what appears to be Cassius's lack of a private life—Cassius's seeming refusal to acknowledge his own sensibilities or nurture his spirit suggest a coldness, a lack of human warmth. Caesar comments to Antony, "He loves no plays, / As thou dost, Antony; he hears no music. / Seldom he smiles, and smiles in such a sort / As if he mocked himself, and scorned his spirit / That could be moved to smile at anything" (I.ii.204–208). Cassius remains merely a public man, without any suggestion of a private self. Such a man, Caesar properly recognizes, is made uncomfortable by others' power.

The question of Caesar's own ambition is raised in Casca's account of the triumphal procession. In describing how Antony offered Caesar a crown three times, Casca makes sure to point out Caesar's reluctance in refusing the crown. Since the incident is related from Casca's anti-Caesar perspective, it is difficult to ascertain Caesar's true motivations: did Caesar act out of genuine humility or did he merely put on a show to please the crowd? Nevertheless, Casca's mention of Caesar's hesitation suggests that, no matter how noble his motivations, Caesar is capable of being seduced by power and thereby capable of becoming a dictator, as Brutus fears.

At the close of the scene, when Cassius plots to turn Brutus against Caesar by planting forged letters in Brutus's house, Cassius has shrewdly perceived that Brutus's internal conflict is more likely to be influenced by what he believes the populace to think than by his own personal misgivings. Cassius recognizes that if Brutus believes that the people distrust Caesar, then he will be convinced that Caesar must be thwarted. Cassius aims to take advantage of

Brutus's weakest point, namely, Brutus's honorable concerns for Rome; Brutus's inflexible ideals leave him open to manipulation by Cassius. Cassius, in contrast, has made himself adaptable for political survival by wholly abandoning his sense of honor.

ACT I, SCENE III

SUMMARY

Casca and Cicero meet on a Roman street. Casca says that though he has seen many terrible things in the natural world, nothing compares to the frightfulness of this night's weather. He wonders if there is strife in heaven or if the gods are so angered by mankind that they intend to destroy it. Casca relates that he saw a man with his hands on fire, and yet his flesh was not burning. He describes meeting a lion near the Capitol: bizarrely, the lion ignored him and walked on. Many others have seen men on fire walking in the streets, and an owl, a nocturnal bird, was seen sitting out in the marketplace during the day. When so many abnormal events happen at once, Casca declares, no one could possibly believe that they are natural occurrences. Casca insists that they are portents of danger ahead. Cicero replies that men will interpret things as they will: "Indeed it is a strange-disposèd time; / But men may construe things after their fashion, / Clean from the purpose of the things themselves" (I.iii.33–35). Cicero asks if Caesar is coming to the Capitol the next day; Casca replies that he is. Cicero departs, warning that it is not a good atmosphere in which to remain outside.

Cassius enters. He has been wandering through the streets, taking no shelter from the thunder and lightning. Casca asks Cassius why he would endanger himself so. Cassius replies that he is pleased—he believes that the gods are using these signs to warn the Romans about a "monstrous state," meaning both an abnormal state of affairs and an atrocious government (I.iii.71). Cassius compares the night to Caesar himself, who

> like this dreadful night,
> . . . thunders, lightens, opens graves, and roars
> As doth the lion in the Capitol.   (I.iii.72–74)

He also calls Caesar "prodigious grown, / And fearful, as these strange eruptions are" (I.iii.76–77).

Casca reports to Cassius that the senators plan to make Caesar king in the Senate the following day. Cassius draws his dagger and swears to the gods that if they can make a weak man like Caesar so powerful, then they can empower Cassius to defeat a tyrant. He declares that Rome must be merely trash or rubbish to give itself up so easily to Caesar's fire. Casca joins Cassius in his censure of Caesar, and Cassius reveals that he has already swayed a number of high-powered Romans to support a resistance movement.

A conspirator named Cinna enters. Cassius now divulges his latest scheme in his plot to build opposition against Caesar: the conversion of Brutus. Cassius gives Cinna the letters he has forged to place in Brutus's chair in the Senate, and others to throw through Brutus's window and place on Brutus's statue. Cassius claims that Brutus has already come three-quarters of the way toward turning against Caesar; he hopes the letters will bring him the rest of the way around. Casca comments that the noble Brutus's participation in their plot will bring worthiness to their schemes, for "he sits high in all the people's hearts, / And that which would appear offence in us / His countenance, like richest alchemy, / Will change to virtue and to worthiness" (I.iii.157–60).

SUMMARY & ANALYSIS

ANALYSIS

This scene demonstrates the characters' inability to interpret correctly the signs that they encounter. The night is full of portents, but no one construes them accurately. Cassius asserts that they signify the danger that Caesar's possible coronation would bring to the state, while they actually warn of the destruction that Cassius himself threatens. Meanwhile, Cassius plots to win Brutus to his cause by misleading him with letters; he knows that Brutus will take the written word at face value, never questioning the letters' authenticity.

The juxtaposition of Cicero's grave warning about not walking in this night's disturbing weather with Cassius's self-satisfied mood upon meeting with Casca (he labels the night "very pleasing . . . to honest men" [I.iii.43]) aligns Cassius with the evil that the omens portend. Further, this nexus suggests a sort of pathetic fallacy—an artistic device by means of which an inanimate entity assumes human emotions and responses (Shakespeare was especially fond of employing pathetic fallacy with nature in moments of turmoil, as in *Macbeth*, when the night grows increasingly eerie until Macbeth observes that "Nature seems dead" right before he goes to murder

King Duncan [II.i.50]). In *Julius Caesar,* the terrifying atmosphere of supernatural phenomena reflects Cassius's horrific plan to murder Caesar.

Furthermore, Cassius not only walks about freely in the atmosphere of terror but relishes it: "And when the cross blue lightning seemed to open / The breast of heaven, I did present myself / Even in the aim and very flash of it" (I.iii.50–52). He insinuates that the "monstrous state" of which the heavens warn refers to Caesar and his overweening ambition, yet he himself has become something of a monster—obsessed with bringing Caesar down, brazenly unafraid of lethal lightning bolts, and haughty about this fearlessness (I.iii.71). As Casca notes, "It is the part of men to fear and tremble" at such ill omens; Cassius seems to have lost his humanity and become a beast (I.iii.54).

The various omens and portents in *Julius Caesar* also raise questions about the force of fate versus free will. The function and meaning of omens in general is puzzling and seemingly contradictory: as *announcements* of an event or events to come, omens appear to prove the existence of some overarching plan for the future, a prewritten destiny controlled by the gods. On the other hand, as *warnings* of impending events, omens suggest that human beings have the power to alter that destiny if provided with the correct information in advance.

ACT II, SCENE I

SUMMARY

Brutus paces back and forth in his garden. He asks his servant to bring him a light and mutters to himself that Caesar will have to die. He knows with certainty that Caesar will be crowned king; what he questions is whether or not Caesar will be corrupted by his power. Although he admits that he has never seen Caesar swayed by power in the past, he believes that it would be impossible for Caesar to reach such heights without eventually coming to scorn those lower in status. Brutus compares Caesar to the egg of a serpent "which, hatched, would as his kind grow mischievous"; thus, he determines to "kill him in the shell" (II.i.33–34).

Brutus's servant enters with a letter that he has discovered near the window. Brutus reads the letter, which accuses him of sleeping while Rome is threatened: "Brutus, thou sleep'st. Awake, and see thyself" (II.i.46). Brutus interprets the letter as a protest against

Caesar: "Thus must I piece it out: / Shall Rome stand under one man's awe?" (II.i.51–52). Believing the people of Rome are telling him their desires through this single letter, he resolves to take the letter's challenge to "speak, strike, redress" (II.i.47). A knock comes at the door. Brutus's servant announces Cassius and a group of men—the conspirators. They include Casca, Decius, Cinna, Metellus, and Trebonius.

Cassius introduces the men, then draws Brutus aside. The two speak briefly before rejoining the others. Cassius suggests that they swear an oath, but Brutus demurs. They have no need for oaths, he says, since their cause should be strong enough to bind them together. The group discusses whether it should try to bring the esteemed Cicero into the conspiracy, for he would bring good public opinion to their schemes, but Brutus dissuades them, pointing out that Cicero would never follow anyone else's ideas. Cassius then suggests that they would do well to kill Antony in addition to Caesar, but Brutus refuses, saying that this would make their plan too bloody. According to Brutus, they only stand against the spirit of Caesar, which he wishes could be destroyed without the necessity of killing the man himself. He says that they should kill him boldly, but not viciously, so that they might be perceived as purging the state rather than as murderers. Cassius replies that he still fears Antony, but Brutus assures him that Antony will be rendered harmless once Caesar is dead.

Cassius states that no one knows whether Caesar will come to the Capitol that day, since the warnings of augurs (seers or soothsayers) after this brutal evening might keep him at home. But Decius assures the others that he will be able to convince Caesar to ignore his superstitions by flattering his bravery. The conspirators depart, Brutus suggesting that they try to behave like actors and hide their true feelings and intentions.

Brutus's wife, Portia, enters the garden. She wonders what has been worrying Brutus, for his behavior has been strange. He says that he has felt unwell. She asks why he refuses to tell her his concerns, insisting that, as his wife, she should be told about his problems and assuring him that she will keep his secrets. Brutus replies that he wishes he were worthy of such an honorable wife. They hear a knock at the door, and Brutus sends her away with a promise to talk to her later.

Ligarius enters, looking sick. He says he would not be sick if he could be sure that Brutus was involved in a scheme in the name of honor. Brutus says that he is. Ligarius rejoices and accompanies Brutus offstage to hear more of the plan.

ANALYSIS

Cassius's words to Brutus in Act I, scene ii have proved powerful in turning him against Caesar: while alone in his garden, Brutus has come to the conclusion that Caesar must be killed. The forged letter has secured this conversion; though it has appeared so mysteriously in his house and tells him exactly what he wants to hear, Brutus never questions its authenticity. He immediately construes the message's cryptic meaning according to his preconceived inclinations: "Thus must I piece it out," he concludes hastily, allowing for no other interpretation of the words (II.i.51). He displays a tragic naïveté, trusting unquestioningly that the letter speaks for the entire Roman populace.

We see now that once Brutus arrives at a belief or proposition, he throws himself into it wholeheartedly. Upon joining Cassius's conspiracy, he takes control of it. He provides his own garden as the conspirators' meeting place and convinces the gathered men not to take an oath, though Cassius would prefer that they do so. Brutus is the one who sends Decius to speak to Caesar at the end of the scene, and it is he who speaks the final words to the conspirators as they depart. So, too, does Brutus overrule Cassius when he suggests that they assassinate Antony along with Caesar. This position, like all of Brutus's actions, stems from a concern for public opinion: Brutus wants the death of Caesar to appear an honorable gesture; if the scheme became too violent, the conspirators would sacrifice any semblance of honor. He insists rather excessively on preserving honor in the conspiracy, saying that in a noble cause one has no need to swear an oath to others: "Do not stain / The even virtue of our enterprise, / Nor th'insuppressive mettle of our spirits, / To think that or our cause or our performance / Did need an oath" (II.i.131–135). Men swear oaths only when they doubt the strength of each other's devotion; to take up oaths now would be to insult the current undertaking and the men involved. It is a rather ironic proposition from Brutus, who has declared loyalty and friendship to Caesar and now casts those commitments aside. Notably, Brutus asks the men not to "stain" the virtue of their scheme, a word that evokes blood; ultimately, they will not be able to avoid staining themselves with Caesar's blood.

Yet, although Brutus appears completely determined in his inter-actions with the conspirators, his inability to confess his thoughts to Portia signifies that he still harbors traces of doubt regarding the legitimacy of his plan. Portia is a symbol of Brutus's private life—a representative of correct intuition and morality—just as Calpurnia is for Caesar in the next scene. Her husband's dismissal of her intu-itions, like Caesar's of Calpurnia's, leads to folly and points to his largest mistake: his decision to ignore his private feelings, loyalties, and misgivings for the sake of a plan that he believes to be for the public good.

ACT II, SCENES II–IV

SUMMARY: ACT II, SCENE II

Caesar wanders through his house in his dressing gown, kept awake by his wife Calpurnia's nightmares. Three times she has called out in her sleep about Caesar's murder. He sends a servant to bid the priests to offer a sacrifice and tell him the results. Calpurnia enters and insists that Caesar not leave the house after so many bad signs. Caesar rebuffs her, refusing to give in to fear. But Calpurnia, who has never heeded omens before, speaks of what happened in the city earlier that night: dead men walked, ghosts wandered the city, a lioness gave birth in the street, and lightning shattered the skies. These signs portend true danger, she says; Caesar cannot afford to ignore them.

Caesar counters that nothing can change the plans of the gods. He deems the signs to apply to the world in general and refuses to believe that they bode ill for him personally. Calpurnia says that the heavens proclaim the death of only great men, so the omens must have to do with him. Caesar replies that while cowards imagine their death frequently, thus dying in their minds several times over, brave men, refusing to dwell on death, die only once. He cannot un-derstand why men fear death, which must come eventually to all.

The servant enters, reporting that the augurs recommend that Caesar stay home. They examined the entrails of an animal and were unable to find a heart—a bad sign. But Caesar maintains that he will not stay home out of fear. Danger cannot affect Caesar, he says. Calpurnia begs him to send Antony to the Senate in his place; finally Caesar relents.

Decius enters, saying that he has come to bring Caesar to the Senate. Caesar tells him to tell the senators that he will be absent that day. Calpurnia tells him to plead illness, but Caesar refuses to lie. Decius then asks what reason he should offer. Caesar states that it is simply his will to stay home. He adds that Calpurnia has had a dream in which she saw his statue run with blood like a fountain, while many smiling Romans bathed their hands in the blood; she has taken this to portend danger for Caesar.

Decius disputes Calpurnia's interpretation, saying that actually the dream signifies that Romans will all gain lifeblood from the strength of Caesar. He confides that the Senate has decided to give Caesar the crown that day; if Caesar were to stay at home, the senators might change their minds. Moreover, Caesar would lose public regard if he were perceived as so easily swayed by a woman, or by fear. Caesar replies that his fears now indeed seem small. He calls for his robe and prepares to depart. Cassius and Brutus enter with Ligarius, Metellus, Casca, Trebonius, and Cinna to escort him to the Senate. Finally, Antony enters. Caesar prepares to depart.

SUMMARY: ACT II, SCENE III

Artemidorus comes onstage, reading to himself a letter that he has written to Caesar, warning him to be wary of Brutus, Casca, and the other conspirators. He stands along the route that Caesar will take to the Senate, prepared to hand the letter to him as he passes. He is sad to think that the virtue embodied by Caesar may be destroyed by the ambitious envy of the conspirators. He remains hopeful, however, that if his letter gets read, Caesar may yet live.

SUMMARY: ACT II, SCENE IV

Portia sends Brutus's servant to the Senate to observe events and report back to her how Caesar is faring. A Soothsayer enters, and Portia asks him if Caesar has gone to the Capitol yet. The Soothsayer replies that he knows that Caesar has not yet gone; he intends to wait for Caesar along his route, since he wants to say a word to him. He goes to the street to wait, hoping that Caesar's entourage will let him speak to the great man.

ANALYSIS: ACT II, SCENES II–IV

These scenes emphasize the many grave signs portending Caesar's death, as well as his stubborn refusal to heed them. Initially, Caesar does agree to stay home in order to please Calpurnia, showing more concern for his wife than Brutus did for Portia in the previous scene. In appreciating Calpurnia's fear, Caesar demonstrates an ability to pay attention to his private matters, albeit a muffled one. But when

Decius tells him that the senators plan to offer him the crown that day, Caesar's desire to comfort his wife gives way to his ambition, and his public self again prevails over his private self.

Increasingly and markedly in these scenes, Caesar refers to himself in the third person, especially when he speaks of his lack of fear ("Yet Caesar shall go forth, for these predictions / Are to the world in general as to Caesar" [II.ii.28–29]). Tragically, he no longer sees the difference between his powerful public image and his vulnerable human body. Even at home in his dressing gown, far from the senators and crowds whose respect he craves, he assumes the persona of "Caesar," the great man who knows no fear. Caesar has displayed a measure of humility in turning down the crown the day before, but this humility has evaporated by the time he enters into his third-person self-commentary and hastens to the Senate to accept the crown at last.

Perhaps this behavior partially confirms the conspirators' charges: Caesar does seem to long for power and would like to hold the crown; he really might become a tyrant if given the opportunity. Whether this speculation constitutes reason sufficient to kill him is debatable. Indeed, it seems possible that the faults that the conspirators—with the possible exception of Brutus—see in Caesar are viewed through the veil of their own ambition: they oppose his kingship not because he would make a poor leader, but because his leadership would preclude their own. In explaining the noble deed to be performed to Ligarius, Brutus describes it as "a piece of work that will make sick men whole." Ligarius responds, "But are not some whole that we must make sick?" (II.i.326–327). Whereas Brutus's primary concern is the well-being of the people, Ligarius's is with bringing down those above him.

Calpurnia's dream of the bleeding statue perfectly foreshadows the eventual unfolding of the assassination plot: the statue is a symbol of Caesar's corpse, and the vague smiling Romans turn out, of course, to be the conspirators, reveling in his bloodshed. Yet, to the end, Caesar remains unconvinced by any omens. If one argues that omens serve as warnings by which individuals can avoid disaster, then one must view Caesar's inflexibility regarding these omens as an arrogance that brings about his death. On the other hand, Shakespeare also imparts Caesar's stubbornness with dignity and a touch of wisdom, as when Caesar professes that since the gods decide the time of one's death, death cannot be averted: if it is fated for the conspirators to kill him, perhaps to die bravely is the most honorable, worthy course of action he can take.

ACT III, SCENE I

But I am constant as the Northern Star,
Of whose true fixed and resting quality
There is no fellow in the firmament.

(See QUOTATIONS, *p. 53)*

SUMMARY

Artemidorus and the Soothsayer await Caesar in the street. Caesar enters with Brutus, Cassius, Casca, Decius, Metellus, Trebonius, Cinna, Ligarius, Antony, and other senators. Artemidorus approaches with his letter, saying that its contents are a matter of closest concern for Caesar. Caesar responds, "What touches us ourself shall be last served"—that is, his personal concerns are his last priority (III.i.8). Artemidorus tells him to read it instantly, but Caesar dismisses him as crazy.

The group enters the Senate, and Cassius worries that the assassination plot has been discovered. Trebonius draws Antony away from the Senate room. Metellus approaches Caesar to request that his brother, Publius Cimber, who has been banished from Rome, be granted permission to return. Caesar answers that since Publius was banished by lawful decree, there is not just cause for absolving his guilt. Brutus and Cassius kneel at Caesar's feet and repeat Metellus's plea; Caesar answers that he will not change his mind now, declaring himself as "constant as the Northern Star" (III.i.60). When Cinna comes forward and kneels to plead further, Caesar adds another comparison, suggesting that they might as well hope to "lift up Olympus," the mountain where the gods were believed to dwell, as to sway Caesar in his convictions (III.i.74).

Decius and Ligarius, followed by Casca, come forward to kneel at Caesar's feet. Casca stabs Caesar first, and the others quickly follow, ending with Brutus. Recognizing that Brutus, too, has joined with the conspirators, Caesar speaks his last words: "*Et tu, Brute?—*Then fall Caesar" (III.i.76). He then yields and dies. The conspirators proclaim the triumph of liberty, and many exit in a tumult, including Lepidus and Artemidorus. Trebonius enters to announce that Antony has fled.

Brutus tells the conspirators that they have acted as friends to Caesar by shortening the time that he would have spent fearing death. He urges them to bend down and bathe their hands in Caesar's blood, then walk to the marketplace (the Roman Forum) with their bloodied swords to proclaim peace, freedom, and liberty. Cassius agrees, declaring that the scene they now enact will be repeated time and again in the ages to come as a commemorative ritual.

Antony's servant enters with a message: Antony, having learned of Caesar's death, sends word that he loved Caesar but will now vow to serve Brutus if Brutus promises not to punish him for his past allegiance. Brutus says that he will not harm Antony and sends the servant to bid him come. Brutus remarks to Cassius that Antony will surely be an ally now, but Cassius replies that he still has misgivings.

Antony enters and sees Caesar's corpse. He marvels at how a man so great in deed and reputation could end as such a small and pathetic body. He tells the conspirators that if they mean to kill him as well, they should do it at once, for there would be no better place to die than beside Caesar. Brutus tells Antony not to beg for death, saying that although their hands appear bloody, their hearts have been, and continue to be, full of pity; although they must appear to him now as having acted in cruelty, their actual motives stemmed from sympathy and love for the Roman populace. Brutus tells Antony to wait until the conspirators have calmed the multitude; then they will explain fully why they have killed Caesar. Antony says he does not doubt their wisdom and shakes each of their bloody hands, staining the not-yet-bloodied hands of Trebonius, who has returned from leading Antony astray, in the process.

Antony now addresses Caesar's departed spirit, asking to be pardoned for making peace with the conspirators over his dead body. After Antony praises Caesar's bravery, Cassius questions his loyalty. Antony assures Cassius that he indeed desires to be numbered among their friends, explaining that he merely forgot himself for a moment upon seeing Caesar's body. He emphasizes that he will gladly ally himself with all of the former conspirators, as long as they can explain to him why Caesar was dangerous.

Brutus assures Antony that he will find their explanation satisfactory. Antony asks if he might bring the body to the Forum and speak a funeral oration. Brutus consents, but Cassius urges him against granting permission. He tells Brutus that Antony will surely move the people against them if he is allowed to speak. Brutus replies that he will preface Antony's words, explaining to the public the reason for the conspirators' deed, and then explain that Antony has been allowed to speak only by Brutus's consent. He believes that the people will admire his magnanimity for allowing Antony, a friend of Caesar's, to take part in the funeral, and that the episode will benefit the conspiracy's public image. Cassius remains displeased, but Brutus allows Antony to take Caesar's body, instructing him to speak well of them since they are doing him a favor by permitting him to give the oration.

All depart; Antony remains alone onstage. He asks Caesar to pardon him for being gentle with his murderers. Antony prophesies that civil strife will follow Caesar's death and lead to much destruction. As long as the foul deed of Caesar's death remains unavenged, he predicts, Caesar's spirit will continue to seek revenge, bringing chaos to Rome.

Octavius's servant enters and sees the body on the ground. Antony tells him to return to Octavius, who had been traveling to Rome at Caesar's behest, and keep his master out of the city; Rome is now dangerous for Octavius, Caesar's adopted son and appointed successor. But Antony urges the servant to come to the Forum and hear his funeral speech. Once they see how the public responds to the conspirators' evil deed, they can decide how Octavius should proceed.

ANALYSIS

Just preceding his death, Caesar refuses Artemidorus's pleas to speak with him, saying that he gives last priority to his nearest, most personal concerns. He thus again demonstrates a split between his public and private selves, endangering himself by believing that his public self is so strong that his private self cannot be harmed. This sense of invulnerability manifests itself clearly when Caesar compares himself to the North Star, which never moves from its position at the center of the sky: "constant as the Northern Star, / Of whose true fixed and resting quality / There is no fellow in the firmament. / [the] one in all [that] doth hold his place" (III.i.60–65). He not only considers himself steadfast but also infallible, beyond the questioning of mortal men, as he compares the foolish idea of him being persuaded of something to the impossible act of hefting the weight of Mount Olympus. In positioning himself thus as a divine figure (the Romans deified certain beloved figures, such as popular leaders, and believed that, upon dying, these figures became ensconced in the firmament), Caesar reveals his belief that he is truly a god. His refusal to pardon Metellus's banished brother serves to show that his belief in the sanctity of his own authority is unwavering up to the moment that he is killed.

Cassius suggests that future generations will remember, repeat, and retell the conspirators' actions in the years to come. The statement constitutes a self-referential moment in the play, since Shakespeare's play itself is a retelling of a retelling: the historical murder of Caesar had been treated earlier by Plutarch (46–119? A.D.), whose *Lives of the Noble Greeks and Romans* served as Shakespeare's source. It was Plutarch who asserted that Caesar ceased to defend himself upon recognizing Brutus among the conspirators, and Plutarch who first gave Caesar his famous last words, which Shakespeare preserves in the original Latin, *"Et tu, Brute?"* ("And you, Brutus?" [III.i.76]). With these words, Caesar apprehends the immensity of the plot to kill him—a plot so total that it includes even his friends—and simultaneously levels a heartbroken reproach at his former friend. By Shakespeare's time, Plutarch's lines had already achieved fame, and an Elizabethan audience would likely have anticipated them in the murder scene.

It is Shakespeare's deft hand of creation, however, that brings Antony to the scene. Despairing over Caesar's death, Antony knows that he poses a danger to the conspirators and that he must pretend to support them if he wants to survive. He assures them that they have his allegiance and shakes their hands, thus smearing himself with Caesar's blood and marking Trebonius with blood as well. By marking Trebonius, Antony may be silently insisting on Trebonius's guilt in the murder, even if his part was less direct than that of the other conspirators. Yet he does so in a handshake, an apparent gesture of allegiance. While the blood on Trebonius's hands marks him as a conspirator, the blood on Antony's hands, like war paint, marks him as the self-appointed instrument for vengeance against Caesar's killers.

Cassius's worries about Antony's rhetorical skill prove justified. The first scene of the play clearly illustrates the fickleness of the multitude, which hastens to cheer Caesar's triumph over a man whom it once adored. Surely the conspirators run a great risk by letting such a fickle audience listen to the mournful Antony. Yet, blinded by his conception of the assassination as a noble deed done for the people and one that the people must thus necessarily appreciate, Brutus believes that the masses will respond most strongly not to Antony's words but to the fact that the conspirators have allowed him to speak at all. Because he feels that he himself, by helping to murder a dear friend, has sacrificed the most, Brutus believes that he will be respected for giving priority to public matters over private ones. We will see, however, that Brutus's misjudgment will lead to his own downfall: he grossly underestimates Antony's oratorical skill and overestimates the people's conception of virtue.

ACT III, SCENES II–III

> *He was my friend, faithful and just to me.*
> *But Brutus says he was ambitious,*
> *And Brutus is an honourable man.*
>
> (See QUOTATIONS, p. 54)

SUMMARY: ACT III, SCENE II

Brutus and Cassius enter the Forum with a crowd of plebeians. Cassius exits to speak to another portion of the crowd. Brutus addresses the onstage crowd, assuring them that they may trust in his honor. He did not kill Caesar out of a lack of love for him, he says, but because his love for Rome outweighed his love of a single man. He insists that Caesar was great but ambitious: it was for this reason that he slew him. He feared that the Romans would live as slaves under Caesar's leadership.

He asks if any disagree with him, and none do. He thus concludes that he has offended no one and asserts that now Caesar's death has been accounted for, with both his virtues and faults in life given due attention. Antony then enters with Caesar's body. Brutus explains to the crowd that Antony had no part in the conspiracy but that he will now be part of the new commonwealth. The plebeians cheer Brutus's apparent kindness, declaring that Brutus should be Caesar. He quiets them and asks them to listen to Antony, who has obtained permission to give a funeral oration. Brutus exits.

Antony ascends to the pulpit while the plebeians discuss what they have heard. They now believe that Caesar was a tyrant and that Brutus did right to kill him. But they wait to hear Antony. He asks the audience to listen, for he has come to bury Caesar, not to praise him. He acknowledges Brutus's charge that Caesar was ambitious and maintains that Brutus is "an honourable man," but he says that Caesar was his friend (III.ii.84). He adds that Caesar brought to Rome many captives, whose countrymen had to pay their ransoms, thus filling Rome's coffers. He asks rhetorically if such accumulation of money for the people constituted ambition. Antony continues that Caesar sympathized with the poor: "When that the poor have cried, Caesar hath wept" (III.ii.88). He reminds the plebeians of the day when he offered the crown to Caesar three times, and Caesar three times refused. Again, he ponders aloud whether this humility constituted ambition. He claims that he is not trying to disprove Brutus's words but rather to tell them what he, Antony, knows; he insists that as they all loved Caesar once, they should mourn for him now.

Antony pauses to weep. The plebeians are touched; they remember when Caesar refused the crown and wonder if more ambitious people have not stepped into his place. Antony speaks again, saying that he would gladly stir them to mutiny and rebellion, though he will not harm Brutus or Cassius, for they are—again—honorable men. He then brings out Caesar's will. The plebeians beg him to read it. Antony says that he should not, for then they would be touched by Caesar's love for them. They implore him to read it. He replies that he has been speaking too long—he wrongs the honorable men who have let him address the crowd. The plebeians call the conspirators traitors and demand that Antony read the will.

Finally, Antony descends from the pulpit and prepares to read the letter to the people as they stand in a circle around Caesar's corpse. Looking at the body, Antony points out the wounds that Brutus and Cassius inflicted, reminding the crowd how Caesar loved Brutus, and yet Brutus stabbed him viciously. He tells how Caesar died and blood ran down the steps of the Senate. Then he uncovers the body for all to see. The plebeians weep and become enraged. Antony says that they should not be stirred to mutiny against such "honourable men" (III.ii.148). He protests that he does not intend to steal away their hearts, for he is no orator like Brutus. He proclaims himself a plain man; he speaks only what he knows, he says—he will let Caesar's wounds speak the rest. If he were Brutus, he claims, he could urge them to rebel, but he is merely Antony.

The people declare that they will mutiny nonetheless. Antony calls to them to let him finish: he has not yet read the will. He now reads that Caesar has bequeathed a sum of money from his personal holdings to every man in Rome. The citizens are struck by this act of generosity and swear to avenge this selfless man's death. Antony continues reading, revealing Caesar's plans to make his private parks and gardens available for the people's pleasure. The plebeians can take no more; they charge off to wreak havoc throughout the city. Antony, alone, wonders what will come of the mischief he has set loose on Rome. Octavius's servant enters. He reports that Octavius

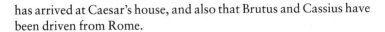

has arrived at Caesar's house, and also that Brutus and Cassius have been driven from Rome.

SUMMARY: ACT III, SCENE III

Cinna the poet, a different man from Cinna the conspirator, walks through the city. A crowd of plebeians descends, asking his name. He answers that his name is Cinna, and the plebeians confuse him with the conspirator Cinna. Despite Cinna's insistence that they have the wrong man, the plebeians drag him off and beat him to death.

ANALYSIS: ACT III, SCENES II–III

Act III, scene ii evidences the power of rhetoric and oratory: first Brutus speaks and then Antony, each with the aim of persuading the crowd to his side. We observe each speaker's effect on the crowd and see the power that words can have—how they can stir emotion, alter opinion, and induce action. Brutus speaks to the people in prose rather than in verse, presumably trying to make his speech seem plain and to keep himself on the level of the plebeians. He quickly convinces the people that Caesar had to die because he would have become a tyrant and brought suffering to them all. He desires to convey that this message comes from the mouth of a concerned Roman citizen, not from the mouth of a greedy usurper.

Antony's speech is a rhetorical tour de force. He speaks in verse and repeats again and again that Brutus and the conspirators are honorable men; the phrase "Brutus says he was ambitious, / And Brutus is an honourable man" accrues new levels of sarcasm at each repetition (III.ii.83–84). Antony answers Brutus's allegation that Caesar was "ambitious" by reminding the crowd of the wealth that Caesar brought to Rome, Caesar's sympathy for the poor, and his refusal to take the throne when offered it—details seeming to disprove any charges of ambition. Pausing to weep openly before the plebeians, he makes them feel pity for him and for his case.

Antony's refined oratorical skill enables him to manipulate the crowd into begging him to read Caesar's will. By means of *praeteritio,* a rhetorical device implemented by a speaker to mention a certain thing while claiming not to mention it, Antony alerts the plebeians to the fact that Caesar cared greatly for them: "It is not meet [fitting] you know how Caesar loved you . . . 'Tis good you know not that you are his heirs" (III.ii.138–142). Under the pretense of sympathetically wanting to keep the plebeians from becoming outraged,

Antony hints to them that they should become outraged. He thus gains their favor.

Further demonstrating his charisma, Antony descends from the pulpit—a more effective way of becoming one with the people than Brutus's strategy of speaking in prose. In placing himself physically among the crowd, Antony joins the commoners without sacrificing his rhetorical influence over them. First he speaks of Caesar's wounds and his horrible death; he shows the body, evoking fully the pity and anger of the crowd. He claims, with false modesty, that he is not a great orator, like Brutus, and that he doesn't intend to incite revolt. Yet in this very sentence he effects the exact opposite of what his words say: he proves himself a deft orator indeed, and although he speaks against mutiny, he knows that at this point the mere mention of the word will spur action.

Having prepared the kindling with his speech, Antony lights the fire of the people's fury with his presentation of Caesar's will. Caesar had intended to share his wealth with the people of Rome and had planned to surrender his parks for their benefit. Antony predicts and utilizes the people's sense of injustice at being stripped of so generous a ruler. The people completely forget their former sympathy for Brutus and rise up against the conspirators, leaving Antony to marvel at the force of what he has done.

In the ensuing riot, the killing of Cinna the poet exemplifies the irrationality of the brutality that has been unleashed; since Caesar's murder, Rome has become so anarchic that even a poet finds himself in grave danger. This murder of the wrong man parallels the conspirators' more metaphoric murder of the wrong man: although Brutus and Cassius believe that they have brought an end to Caesar's charisma and authority, they have merely brought an end to the mortal body that he inhabited. While the body may lie dead, the true Caesar, the leader of the people, lives on in their hearts—as he does in the anxious minds of the conspirators: Brutus will soon encounter Caesar's ghost near the battlefield. The populace will now seek a man who can serve as their "Caesar"—the word has now become a synonym for "ruler"—in his place; Caesar has instilled in the Romans a desire to replace the old republic with a monarchy.

ACT IV, SCENES I–II

> *He must be taught, and trained, and bid go forth —*
> *A barren-spirited fellow . . .*
> *. . . a property.*
>
> *(See* QUOTATIONS, *p. 55)*

SUMMARY: ACT IV, SCENE I

Antony meets Octavius and Lepidus at his house. They review a list of names, deciding who must be killed. Lepidus agrees to the death of his brother if Antony will agree to allow his nephew to be killed. Antony suggests that, as a way of saving money, they examine Caesar's will to see if they can redirect some of his funds. Lepidus departs, and Antony asks Octavius if Lepidus is a worthy enough man to rule Rome with him and Octavius. Octavius replies that he trusts him, but Antony harbors doubts. Octavius points out that Lepidus is a "tried and valiant soldier," to which Antony responds, "So is my horse": he goes on to compare Lepidus to a mere animal, calling him a "barren-spirited fellow" and a mere tool (IV.i.28–36). Antony now turns the conversation to Brutus and Cassius, who are reportedly gathering an army; it falls to Octavius and Antony to confront them and halt their bid for power.

> *There is a tide in the affairs of men*
> *. . .*
> *And we must take the current when it serves . . .*
>
> *(See* QUOTATIONS, *p. 56)*

SUMMARY: ACT IV, SCENE II

Meanwhile, Brutus waits with his men in camp and meets with Lucillius, Titinius, and Pindarus. Lucillius bears a message from Cassius and steps aside to speak to Brutus. He says that Cassius is becoming more and more displeased with Brutus, and Brutus worries that their ties may be weakening. Cassius arrives with his army and accuses Brutus of having wronged him. Brutus replies that he would not wrong him, as he considers him his brother, and insists that they continue the discussion privately in Brutus's tent.

Cassius charges Brutus with having condemned one of their men for taking bribes, even though Cassius sent letters asking him not to, since Cassius knew the man. Brutus responds by accusing Cassius of having taken bribes himself at times. Brutus tells him to recall the Ides of March, when they killed Caesar because they believed that he was corrupt. He asks Cassius if they should now allow themselves to descend into the very corruption that they tried to eliminate. Cassius tells Brutus not to bait him any more, for Cassius is a soldier and will fight.

The two men insult each other, and Brutus expresses the reasons for his disappointment in Cassius. Because he claims to be so honest himself that he cannot raise money by ignoble means, he was forced to ask Cassius for money, but Cassius ignored him. Cassius claims that he did not deny Brutus, but that the messenger misreported Brutus's words. Cassius accuses Brutus of having ceased to love him. He hopes that Antony and Octavius will kill him soon, for, having lost his closest ally and friend, he no longer desires to live. He offers his dagger to Brutus to kill him, declaring, "Strike as thou didst at Caesar; for I know / When though didst hate him worst, thou loved'st him better / Than ever thou loved'st Cassius" (IV.ii.159–161).

Brutus tells Cassius to put his dagger away and says that they both are merely ill-tempered. The two men embrace and forgive each other. Outside, Lucillius is attempting to prevent a poet from entering the tent, but the poet squeezes past him and scolds Brutus and Cassius for arguing: "Love and be friends, as two such men should be, / For I have seen more years, I'm sure, than ye" (IV.ii.183–184). But, having already repledged their friendship, the two generals laugh together at the poet's presumptuousness and send him away.

Cassius and Brutus drink wine together. Cassius expresses his surprise at Brutus's earlier rage. Brutus explains that he has been under many emotional burdens lately, the foremost of which has been the death of his wife, Portia; he recently received news that she killed herself by swallowing fire. Titinius and Messala enter with news from Rome; Messala says that the triumvirate of Octavius, Antony, and Lepidus has put a hundred senators to death. Messala asks Brutus if he has had word from Portia, and when Brutus answers negatively, Messala comments that this seems strange. When Brutus inquires if Messala knows something, Messala replies that he does not. But Brutus insists that Messala tell him the truth, and Messala reports that Portia is dead.

Brutus suggests that they march to Philippi to meet the enemy. Cassius says that he would rather let the enemy come to them. Brutus protests that they are at the peak of their readiness and should seize the opportunity. Cassius relents and agrees to march. The others depart, leaving Brutus in his tent with his servant Lucius. Brutus sum-

mons Varro and Claudio to sleep in his tent until they are needed for
early morning messages.

The others fall asleep while Brutus lies awake trying to read. A
spectral image enters (identified in the text as "Ghost of Caesar").
Brutus wonders if he is dreaming; he asks the form to identify himself. The Ghost replies that he is "thy evil spirit" (IV.ii.333). After
telling Brutus that they will see each other again at Philippi, the
Ghost disappears, and Brutus wakes his attendants. He asks them if
they saw anything strange, but they reply that they did not.

ANALYSIS: ACT IV, SCENES I–II

These scenes deal with the events that take place in the vacuum of
power left by Caesar's death. Antony's speech to the Roman citizens in Act III, scene ii centers on the fact that Caesar had set aside
money for each citizen. Now, ironically, he searches for ways to
turn these funds into cash in order to raise an army against Brutus
and Cassius. Although he has gained his current power by offering
to honor Caesar's will and provide the citizens with their rightful
money, we now see that he apparently has no intention of fulfilling
this promise. In a strange dialogue with Octavius, he also badly
insults Lepidus, explaining how, just as his horse has been taught
to fight, turn, stop, and move his body according to Antony's will,
so, too, must Lepidus now be trained. Antony declares Lepidus "a
barren-spirited fellow, one that feeds / On objects, arts, and imitations"; he reproaches Octavius, saying, "Do not talk of him / But as
a property," that is, as a mere instrument for the furtherance of their
own goals (IV.i.36–40). Lepidus proves an effective tool for them in
that he is malleable and apparently not intelligent enough to devise
his own motives. While Shakespeare may have inserted this string
of insults simply for comic relief, this abuse serves as another illustration of Antony's sense of political expediency: while he does not
respect Lepidus, he still uses him for his own purposes.

Meanwhile, questions of honor plague the conspirators as well,
as Cassius and Brutus exchange accusations. Their argument seems
to arise partially from a misunderstanding but also partially from
stubbornness. Though Brutus claims that his honor forbids him
from raising money in unscrupulous ways, he would still use such
money as long as it was not he himself, but rather Cassius, who
raised it. We see that Brutus speaks against corruption, but when
he has no other means of paying his army, he quickly consents to
unscrupulousness, if only indirectly.

Portia's death is reported twice in scene ii (Plutarch's telling, upon which Shakespeare based his play, describes Portia's death more explicitly: she put hot coals in her mouth and choked herself to death). Some argue that the repetition of the announcement of Portia's suicide reveals the effect of revision on Shakespeare's part; perhaps, while adding in one section of the scene, he forgot to re-move another. Other scholars suggest that Brutus's two separate comments regarding Portia's death show two separate sides of his personality—again, the private versus the public. That is, alone with Cassius, he admits his distress at the loss of his wife, but before his men, he appears indifferent or dispassionate. Perhaps the latter reaction is merely a façade, and Brutus simply has too much pride to show his true feelings in public.

Brutus's words to Cassius proclaiming their readiness for battle are significant in that they emphasize Brutus's belief in the power of the will over fate:

> We at the height are ready to decline.
> There is a tide in the affairs of men
> Which, taken at the flood, leads on to fortune;
> Omitted, all the voyage of their life
> Is bound in shallows and in miseries.
> On such a full sea are we now afloat,
> And we must take the current when it serves,
> Or lose our ventures.   (IV.ii.269–276)

Throughout the play, the theme of fate versus free will proves im-portant: here, Brutus suggests that both exist and that one should take advantage of fate by asserting one's will. While subsequent events demonstrate that the force of fate (or perhaps just Antony and Octavius's superior maneuvering) is stronger than Brutus's in-dividual actions, his speech still makes for a graceful, philosophic axiom, showing Brutus to be a man of deep reflection.

Brutus cannot sleep—perhaps because he is brooding internally on his guilt; in any case, this guilt is soon manifested externally in the form of the Ghost of Caesar. This phantom's identification of him-self to Brutus as "thy evil spirit" could mean either that the Ghost is an evil spirit appearing to Brutus's eyes only—a spirit that is "his" alone—or that the Ghost represents Brutus's own spirit, which is secretly evil (IV.ii.333). However one interprets the arrival of the specter, the event can only bode ill for Brutus in the battle to come.

ACT V, SCENES I–III

SUMMARY: ACT V, SCENE I

Octavius and Antony enter the battlefield at Philippi with their armies. A messenger arrives to report that the enemy is ready for battle. Antony, the more experienced soldier, tells Octavius to attack from the left. Octavius refuses and replies that he will attack from the right and Antony can come from the left. Antony asks Octavius why he questions his authority, but Octavius stands firm.

The enemy factions—consisting of Brutus, Cassius, and their armies—enter; Titinius, Lucillius, and Messala are among them. Octavius asks Antony if their side should attack first, and Antony, now calling Octavius "Caesar," responds that they will wait for the enemy to attack. Antony and Octavius go to meet Brutus and Cassius. The leaders exchange insults. Octavius draws his sword and calls for Caesar's death to be avenged; he swears that he will not lay the sword down again until another Caesar (namely himself) adds the deaths of the traitors to the general slaughter. The leaders insult each other further before parting to ready their armies for battle.

After the departure of Antony and Octavius, Brutus calls Lucillius to talk privately. Cassius calls Messala to do the same. Cassius tells the soldier that it is his birthday and informs him of recent bad omens: two mighty eagles alighted on the foremost banners of their army and perched there, feeding from the soldiers' hands; this morning, however, they are gone. Now ravens, crows, and other scavenger birds circle over the troops as if the men were diseased and weak prey. Cassius walks back to join Brutus and comments that the future looks uncertain; if they lose, they may never see each other again. Cassius asks Brutus if Brutus would allow himself to be led through Rome as a captive should they lose. Brutus replies that he would rather die than go to Rome as a defeated prisoner; he declares that this day "must end that work the ides of March begun"—that is, the battle represents the final stage in the struggle for power that began with the murder of Caesar (V.i.114). He bids Cassius "for ever and for ever farewell" (V.i.117). Cassius echoes these sentiments, and the men depart.

SUMMARY: ACT V, SCENE II

The battle begins between the scenes, and the next scene, comprising a scant total of six lines, depicts the two sides' first surge against each other. Brutus sends Messala to Cassius to report that he senses a weakness in Octavius's army and will push forward to exploit it.

SUMMARY: ACT V, SCENE III

The next scene finds Cassius standing on a hill with Titinius, watching the battle and lamenting its course. Though Brutus was correct in noting Octavius's weakness, he proved overeager in his attack, and the tide of battle has turned against him. Pindarus now runs up to Cassius with a report: Antony's troops have entered Cassius's camp. He advises Cassius to flee to some more distant spot. Cassius refuses to move but, catching sight of a group of burning tents, asks if those tents are his. Titinius confirms that they are. Cassius then notices a series of advancing troops in the distance; he gives Titinius his horse and instructs him to find out whose troops they are. Titinius obeys and rides off.

Cassius asks Pindarus to ascend a nearby hill and monitor Titinius's progress. Pindarus calls down his reports: Titinius, riding hard, is soon surrounded by the unknown men; he dismounts the horse and the unknown men cheer. Distraught at this news of what he takes to be his best friend's capture, Cassius tells Pindarus to watch no more. Pindarus descends the hilltop, whereupon Cassius gives Pindarus his sword, covers his own eyes, and asks Pindarus to kill him. Pindarus complies. Dying, Cassius's last words are that Caesar has now been revenged by the very sword that killed him.

Unexpectedly, Titinius now enters with Messala, observing that the battle rages on without sign of ending. Although Antony's forces defeated those of Cassius, Brutus's legions rallied to defeat those of Octavius. The men then discover Cassius's body. Titinius realizes what has happened: when he rode out to the unknown troops, he discovered the troops to be Brutus's; the men's embrace of Titinius must have appeared to Pindarus a capture, and Cassius must have misperceived their joyful cheers of reunion as the bloodthirsty roars of the enemy's men. Messala departs to bring the tragic news to Brutus. Titinius mourns over Cassius's body, anguished that a man whom he greatly admired died over such a mistake. Miserable, Titinius stabs himself and dies.

Brutus now enters with Messala and his men. Finding the bodies, Brutus cries, "O Julius Caesar, thou art mighty yet": even in death, Caesar is reaping revenge; he seems to turn events against his murderers from beyond the grave (V.iii.93). Brutus orders that Cassius's body be taken away, and the men set off to struggle again with the armies of Antony and Octavius.

ANALYSIS: ACT V, SCENE I–III

When Octavius refuses to agree to Antony's strategic instructions before the battle, his obstinate resolution to follow his own will and his clarity of command echo Caesar's first appearance in the play. In Act I, scene ii, Antony comments, "When Caesar says 'Do this,' it is performed"; such authority is the mark of a powerful leader (I.ii.12). Octavius, Caesar's chosen successor, now has this authority too—his word equals action. Antony, noticing this similarity between adopted son and father, begins calling Octavius "Caesar." Just as Caesar transforms his name from that of a mere mortal into that of a divine figure, Antony converts "Caesar," once one man's name, into the generic title for the ruler of Rome. In at least one way, then, Caesar's permanence is established.

The exchange among the four leaders profits from close reading, as it compares the respective powers of words and swords to harm. When Brutus insists that "good words are better than bad strokes," Antony replies, "In your bad strokes, Brutus, you give good words. / Witness the hole you made in Caesar's heart, / Crying 'Long live, hail Caesar'" (V.i.29–32). Antony suggests that Brutus's use of rhetoric has been just as damaging to Rome as his physical blows, for by falsely swearing allegiance to Caesar he deceived and betrayed him—hypocritically, he murdered Caesar even as he cheered in support of him. Cassius returns the insult by comparing Antony's words to an annoying bee's buzzing, and Antony condemns Cassius and Brutus as "flatterers" (V.i.45). The politicians engage in a skillful rhetorical skirmish, but, ultimately, their words have no effective power. Since Brutus's actions have proved his words treacherous and untrustworthy, the murder of Caesar can now be answered only in blood.

The tragic circumstances of Cassius's death represent another instance of misinterpretation. They refer strongly to Caesar's death: like Caesar, Cassius dies after failing to perceive the truth; and he dies from his own sword, the same sword that killed Caesar. Indeed, the entire scene attests to Caesar's continuing power of influence from beyond the grave: as Cassius dies, he credits the murdered leader with his defeat. Brutus, with the ghostly visitor of the previous night fresh in his mind, also interprets Cassius's death as the doings of a vengeful Caesar. In believing himself immortal, Caesar opened himself up to his murder by the conspirators, and his death seemed to disprove his faith in his own permanence. Yet now the power of Caesar appears to linger on, as events unfold in exact compliance with what Caesar would have wished.

Just as the misinformation that causes Cassius to commit suicide cheapens his death, so too do the manner and consequence of his death render it less noble. Cassius desires a virtuous death, and he believes that dying out of respect and sympathy for his captured friend will afford him just such an end: "O coward that I am, to live so long / To see my best friend ta'en before my face!" (V.iii.34–35). He cannot, however, bring himself to perform the necessary act; though he implies that his choice to die is brave, he does not possess the requisite bravery. Cassius's last line widens this gap between his conception and reality: "Caesar, thou art revenged, / Even with the sword that killed thee" (V.iii.44–45). Cassius attempts to situate his death as a righteous, even graceful, working of dignified fate, and perhaps even to compare himself to the great Caesar. Yet while the sword that kills both is, fatefully, the same, the hands that drive it are not, ruining Cassius's parallel. Immediately after Cassius's death, no dedicated friend delivers a praise-filled, tearful eulogy celebrating his life. Rather, the only witness, Pindarus, a lowly slave, flees to his freedom, "where never Roman shall take note of him" (V.iii.49). Pindarus's idea of escaping notice reflects upon Cassius and his ignoble deeds, for which history will not remember him kindly.

Act V, scenes iv–v

Summary: Act V, scene iv
Brutus prepares for another battle with the Romans. In the field, Lucillius pretends that he is Brutus, and the Romans capture him. Antony's men bring him before Antony, who recognizes Lucillius. Antony orders his men to go see if the real Brutus is alive or dead and to treat their prisoner well.

Summary: Act V, scene v
Brutus sits with his few remaining men. He asks them to hold his sword so that he may run against it and kill himself. The Ghost of Caesar has appeared to him on the battlefield, he says, and he believes that the time has come for him to die. His men urge him to flee; he demurs, telling them to begin the retreat, and that he will catch up later. He then asks one of his men to stay behind and hold the sword so that he may yet die honorably. Impaling himself on the sword, Brutus declares that in killing himself he acts on motives twice as pure as those with which he killed Caesar, and that Caesar

should consider himself avenged: "Caesar, now be still. / I killed not thee with half so good a will" (V.v.50–51).

Antony enters with Octavius, Messala, Lucillius, and the rest of their army. Finding Brutus's body, Lucillius says that he is glad that his master was not captured alive. Octavius decides to take Brutus's men into his own service. Antony speaks over the body, stating that Brutus was the noblest Roman of all: while the other conspirators acted out of envy of Caesar's power, Brutus acted for what he believed was the common good. Brutus was a worthy citizen, a rare example of a real man. Octavius adds that they should bury him in the most honorable way and orders the body to be taken to his tent. The men depart to celebrate their victory.

ANALYSIS: ACT V, SCENES IV–V

Brutus preserves his noble bravery to the end: unlike the cowardly Cassius, who has his slave stab him while he, Cassius, covers his face, Brutus decides calmly on his death and impales himself on his own sword. Upon giving up the ghost, Brutus, like Cassius, addresses Caesar in an acknowledgment that Caesar has been avenged; whereas Cassius closes with a factual remark about Caesar's murder ("Even with the sword that killed thee" [V.iii.45]), Brutus closes with an emotional expression that reveals how his inextinguishable inner conflict has continued to plague him: "I killed not thee with half so good a will" (V.v.51). Additionally, whereas the dead Cassius is immediately abandoned by a lowly slave, the dead Brutus is almost immediately celebrated by his enemy as the noblest of Romans. Notably, Brutus is also the only character in the play to interpret correctly the signs auguring his death. When the Ghost of Caesar appears to him on the battlefield, he unflinchingly accepts his defeat and the inevitability of his death.

With Antony's speech over Brutus's body, the identity of the true hero—albeit a tragic hero—of the play becomes clear. Although Caesar gives the play its name, he has few lines and dies early in the third act. While Octavius has proven himself the leader of the future, he has not yet demonstrated his full glory. History tells us that Antony will soon be ousted from the triumvirate by Octavius's growing power. Over the course of the play, Cassius rises to some power, but since he lacks integrity, he is little more than a petty schemer. The idealistic, tormented Brutus, struggling between his love for Caesar and his belief in the ideal of a republic, faces the most difficult of decisions—a decision in which the most is at stake—and he chooses wrongly. As Antony observes, Brutus's decision to enter into the conspiracy does not originate in ambition but rather in his inflexible belief in what the Roman government should be. His ideal proves too rigid in the political world of the play, in which it appears that one succeeds only through chameleon-like adaptability, through bargaining and compromise—skills that Antony masterfully displays.

Brutus's mistake lies in his attempt to impose his private sense of honor on the whole Roman state. In the end, killing Caesar does not stop the Roman republic from becoming a dictatorship, for Octavius assumes power and becomes a new Caesar. Brutus's beliefs may be a holdover from earlier ideas of statesmanship. Unable to shift into the new world order, Brutus misunderstands Caesar's intentions and mistakes the greedy ambition of the conspirators for genuine civic concern. Thus, Brutus kills his friend and later dies himself. But in the end, Antony, the master rhetorician, with no trace of the sarcasm that suffuses his earlier speech about Brutus, still honors him as the best Roman of them all.

IMPORTANT QUOTATIONS EXPLAINED

1.   I could be well moved if I were as you.
      If I could pray to move, prayers would move me.
      But I am constant as the Northern Star,
      Of whose true fixed and resting quality
      There is no fellow in the firmament.
      The skies are painted with unnumbered sparks;
      They are all fire, and every one doth shine;
      But there's but one in all doth hold his place. (III.i.58–65)

These lines come from Caesar's speech in Act III, scene i, just before his assassination. The conspirators have come to Caesar in the Senate under the pretense of pleading for amnesty for Metellus's banished brother, Publius Cimber. Caesar replies that he will adhere to his word and not change his earlier decision.

Comparing himself to the North Star, Caesar boasts of his constancy, his commitment to the law, and his refusal to waver under any persuasion. This comparison implies more than steadfastness, however: the North Star is the star by which sailors have navigated since ancient times, the star that guides them in their voyages, just as Caesar leads the Roman people. So, too, is the North Star unique in its fixedness; as the only star that never changes its position in the sky, it has "no fellow in the firmament." Thus, Caesar also implies that he is peerless among Romans. Caesar declares that he alone remains "unassailable" among men, and his strictness in Publius Cimber's case illustrates this virtue.

As it comes mere moments before the murder, the speech adds much irony to the scene: having just boasted that he is "unassailable," Caesar is shortly assailed and killed. In announcing his "constancy," Caesar claims permanency—even immortality. The assassins quickly prove Caesar mortal, however. But as the later events of the play reveal, Caesar's influence and eternality are undeniable. His ghost seems to live on to avenge the murder: Brutus and Cassius directly attribute much of their misfortune to Caesar's workings from beyond the grave; so, too, does the name "Caesar" undergo metamorphosis from an individual man's name to the title of an institution—the empiric rule of Rome—by the end of the play. In these more important ways, Caesar's lofty estimation of himself proves true.

2. He was my friend, faithful and just to me.
   But Brutus says he was ambitious,
   And Brutus is an honourable man.
   . . .
   When that the poor have cried, Caesar hath wept.
   . . .
   Yet Brutus says he was ambitious,
   And Brutus is an honourable man.
   . . .
   I thrice presented him a kingly crown,
   Which he did thrice refuse. Was this ambition?
   Yet Brutus says he was ambitious,
   And sure he is an honourable man.   (III.ii.82–96)

Antony speaks these lines in his funeral oration for Caesar in Act III, scene ii. He has asked Brutus's permission to make the speech, and Brutus foolishly allows him the privilege, believing that the boost in image that he and the conspirators will receive for this act of apparent magnanimity will outweigh any damage that Antony's words might do. Unfortunately for the conspirators, Antony's speech is a rhetorical tour de force, undermining the conspirators even while it appears deferential to them. This clever strategy recalls the previous scene (III.i), in which Antony shook hands with each of the murderers in turn, thus smearing Caesar's blood among all of them; while appearing to make a gesture of reconciliation, he silently marked them all as guilty. In both the handshake and the speech, Antony damns the murderers while appearing to pay respect, showing his consummate skill as a politician and rhetorician.

The speech draws much of its power from repetition. Each time Antony cites Brutus's claim that Caesar was "ambitious," the claim loses force and credibility. Similarly, each time Antony declares how "honourable" a man Brutus is, the phrase accrues an increasingly sarcastic tone until, by the end of the speech, its meaning has been completely inverted. The speech wins over the crowd and turns public opinion against the conspirators; when Antony reads Caesar's will aloud a few moments later, the dead Caesar's words join with Antony's in rousing the masses against the injustice of the assassination.

3. [My horse] is a creature that I teach to fight,
   To wind, to stop, to run directly on,
   His corporal motion governed by my spirit;
   And in some taste is Lepidus but so.
   He must be taught, and trained, and bid go forth—
   A barren-spirited fellow, one that feeds
   On objects, arts, and imitations,
   Which, out of use and staled by other men,
   Begin his fashion. Do not talk of him
   But as a property.   (IV.i.31–40)

In this passage from Act IV, scene i, in which Antony and Octavius (with Lepidus, who has just left the room) are making plans to retake Rome, the audience gains insight into Antony's cynicism regarding human nature: while he respects certain men, he considers Lepidus a mere tool, or "property," whose value lies in what other men may do with him and not in his individual human dignity. Comparing Lepidus to his horse, Antony says that the general can be trained to fight, turn, stop, or run straight—he is a mere body subject to the will of another.

The quote raises questions about what qualities make for an effective or valuable military man, politician, and ally. Antony remarks that Lepidus "feeds / On objects, arts, and imitations, / Which, out of use and staled by other men, / Begin his fashion." By this criticism he means that Lepidus centers his life on insubstantial things, prizing what other men have long since discarded as "stale" or devoid of flavor and interest; that is, Lepidus lacks his own will and convictions.

While Lepidus's weak sense of selfhood means that he can easily be used as a tool by other men, it also means that he can be counted on to be obedient and loyal. Lepidus is thus absorbed into the threesome (with Antony and Octavius) that rules Rome after Caesar's death, ultimately coming into power and political prestige with little effort or sacrifice. In *Julius Caesar*, men such as Brutus and Caesar are punished in the mortal realm for their inflexible commitment to specific ideals. Though Antony criticizes Lepidus, perhaps Shakespeare is subtly suggesting that a man such as Lepidus, "barren-spirited" and seemingly lacking in ambition, will be as satisfied in the political realm as his more directed counterparts.

QUOTATIONS

4.   We at the height are ready to decline.
       There is a tide in the affairs of men
       Which, taken at the flood, leads on to fortune;
       Omitted, all the voyage of their life
       Is bound in shallows and in miseries.
       On such a full sea are we now afloat,
       And we must take the current when it serves,
       Or lose our ventures.   (IV.ii.269–276)

Brutus speaks these words in Act IV, scene ii in order to convince Cassius that it is time to begin the battle against Octavius and Antony. He speaks figuratively of a "tide" in the lives of human beings: if one takes advantage of the high tide, one may float out to sea and travel far; if one misses this chance, the "voyage" that one's life comprises will remain forever confined to the shallows, and one will never experience anything more glorious than the mundane events in this narrow little bay. Brutus reproaches Cassius that if they do not "take the current" now, when the time is right, they will lose their "ventures," or opportunities.

The passage elegantly formulates a complex conception of the interplay between fate and free will in human life. Throughout the play, the reader must frequently contemplate the forces of fate versus free will and ponder whether characters might be able to prevent tragedy if they could only understand and heed the many omens that they encounter. This musing brings up further questions, such as whether one can achieve success through virtue, ambition, courage, and commitment, or whether one is simply fated to succeed or fail, with no ability to affect this destiny. Here, Brutus conceives of life as influenced by *both* fate and free will: human beings must be shrewd enough to recognize when fate offers them an opportunity and bold enough to take advantage of it. Thus, Brutus believes, does man achieve a delicate and valuable balance between fate and free will.

This philosophy seems wise; it contains a certain beauty as well, suggesting that while we do not have total control over our lives, we do have a responsibility to take what few measures we can to live nobly and honorably. The only problem, as the play illustrates over and over again, is that it is not always so easy to recognize these nudges of fate, be they opportunities or warnings. The characters' repeated failures to interpret signs correctly and to adapt themselves to events as they unfold form the basis for most of the tragedy that occurs in the play.

KEY FACTS

FULL TITLE
The Tragedy of Julius Caesar

AUTHOR
William Shakespeare

TYPE OF WORK
Play

GENRE
Tragic drama, historical drama

LANGUAGE
English

TIME AND PLACE WRITTEN
1599, in London

DATE OF FIRST PUBLICATION
Published in the First Folio of 1623, probably from the theater company's official promptbook rather than from Shakespeare's manuscript

PUBLISHER
Edward Blount and William Jaggard headed the group of five men who undertook the publication of Shakespeare's First Folio

NARRATOR
None

CLIMAX
Cassius's death (V.iii), upon ordering his servant, Pindarus, to stab him, marks the point at which it becomes clear that the murdered Caesar has been avenged, and that Cassius, Brutus, and the other conspirators have lost in their attempt to keep Rome a republic rather than an empire. Ironically, the conspirators' defeat is not yet as certain as Cassius believes, but his death helps bring about defeat for his side.

PROTAGONISTS
Brutus and Cassius

ANTAGONISTS
Antony and Octavius

SETTING (TIME)
44 B.C.

SETTING (PLACE)
Ancient Rome, toward the end of the Roman republic

POINT OF VIEW
The play sustains no single point of view; however, the audience acquires the most insight into Brutus's mind over the course of the action.

FALLING ACTION
Titinius's realization that Cassius has died wrongly assuming defeat; Titinius's suicide; Brutus's discovery of the two corpses; the final struggle between Brutus's men and the troops of Antony and Octavius; Brutus's self-impalement on his sword upon recognizing that his side is doomed; the discovery of Brutus's body by Antony and Octavius

TENSE
Present

FORESHADOWING
The play is full of omens, including lightning and thunder, the walking dead, and lions stalking through the city (I.iii). Additionally, the Soothsayer warns Caesar to beware the Ides of March (I.ii); Calpurnia dreams that she sees Caesar's statue running with blood (II.ii); and Caesar's priests sacrifice animals to the gods only to find that the animals lack hearts (II.ii)—all foreshadow Caesar's impending murder and the resulting chaos in Rome. Caesar's ghost visits Brutus prior to the battle (IV.ii), and birds of prey circle over the battlefield in sight of Cassius (V.i); both incidents foreshadow Caesar's revenge and the victory of Antony and Octavius.

TONE
Serious, proud, virtuous, enraged, vengeful, idealistic, anguished

THEMES
Fate versus free will; public self versus private self; misinterpretation and misreading of signs and events;

commitment to ideals versus adaptability and compromise; the relationship between rhetoric and power; allegiance and rivalry among men

MOTIFS

Omens and portents, letters

SYMBOLS

The women in the play, Portia and Calpurnia, symbolize the neglected private lives of their respective husbands, Brutus and Caesar. The men dismiss their wives as hindrances to their public duty, ignoring their responsibilities to their own mortal bodies and their private obligations as friends, husbands, and feeling men.

Study Questions

1. *Discuss the attention paid (or not paid) to omens, nightmares, and other supernatural events. What do the various responses to these phenomena show about the struggle between fate and free will in Julius Caesar? Can the play's tragedies be attributed to the characters' failure to read the omens properly, or do the omens merely presage the inevitable?*

The characters in *Julius Caesar* neglect nearly universally the play's various omens (dead men walking, sacrificed animals who lack hearts), nightmares (Calpurnia's vision of Caesar's statue running with blood), warnings (the Soothsayer's advice to Caesar to avoid the Ides of March, Artemidorus's letter about the conspiracy), and supernatural events (Brutus's visitation by the Ghost). Caesar believes that the omens in Rome could apply just as easily to Rome in general as to him personally, and he quickly comes to believe that Calpurnia has misinterpreted her dream. As the plot unfolds, it becomes clear that these omens warn of events that take place without exception. The hand of fate, or of the gods, appears to strike with undeniable omnipotence; and yet, it seems peculiar to provide omens without allowing individuals time to alter their behavior or choose among fates. In any case, the characters fail to heed the warnings in almost every instance. Tragically, the characters often believe that their refusal to heed these signs proves their strength, courage, and indomitable nature; thus, Caesar believes that he is displaying the force of his will by ignoring the warnings and attending the Senate, though, ironically, it is precisely this action that precipitates his fated death.

2.   *Think about Caesar the mortal man as opposed to*
      Caesar the public figure. How does he continue to
      wield power over events even after he is dead? Do the
      conspirators succeed in their goals by killing him, or is
      Caesar's influence too powerful to be contained even
      by his death?

The conspirators manage to kill Caesar, the physically infirm man, who is deaf in one ear, probably epileptic, and aging; indeed, it may be Caesar's delusions about his own immortality as a man that allow the conspirators to catch him off-guard and bring about his death. In many ways, however, Caesar's faith in his permanence proves valid: the conspirators fail to destroy Caesar's public image, and Antony's words to the crowd serve to burnish Caesar's image. Additionally, the conspirators fail to annihilate the idea that Caesar incarnated: that of a single supreme leader of Rome.

Death does not diminish Caesar's influence on matters or his presence in the minds of those who loved him. Caesar seems to speak from the grave when Antony reads his will, stirring the people to rebellion. Cassius and Brutus attribute their deaths to Caesar when they fall in battle. Perhaps most important, Antony begins to call Octavius "Caesar" when Octavius starts to display an undeniable authority in military strategizing. This appellation has a double significance: it reveals both Octavius's future as the bearer of Caesar's personal legacy and the metamorphosis of Caesar the man into Caesar the institution. Even with his death, Caesar has initiated a line of Roman emperors, ending the era of Brutus's beloved republic.

3. *As Caesar's appointed successor, how does Octavius carry on the great general's legacy? Consider his use of language and commands as well as the ways in which the other characters regard him and refer to him.*

Early in the play, Caesar gives an order to Antony, who declares that Caesar is so powerful that words equal action by the mere fact of his having pronounced them. After Caesar's death, words cease to have this kind of absolute power until Octavius arrives on the battlefield. When Antony tells him to attack from one side of the field, Octavius announces his intention to do the opposite. Like Caesar, Octavius is able to effect his will merely by speaking. Antony's earlier recognition of Caesar's power epitomizes one of the driving forces behind this power—the self-fulfilling prophecy of believing in Caesar's supremacy. As a public figure, Caesar depends on the acceptance and awe of those over whom he rules to sustain the legendary, godlike aura surrounding him. With little resistance, Antony submits to Octavius's notion of how they should proceed in battle. This recognition of Octavius's inherently supreme nature and the consequent deference it inspires cements Octavius's status as the emerging successor to Caesar's great legacy. It is at this moment, notably, that Antony begins to call Octavius "Caesar."

STUDY QUESTIONS

How to Write Literary Analysis

The Literary Essay: A Step-by-Step Guide

When you read for pleasure, your only goal is enjoyment. You might find yourself reading to get caught up in an exciting story, to learn about an interesting time or place, or just to pass time. Maybe you're looking for inspiration, guidance, or a reflection of your own life. There are as many different, valid ways of reading a book as there are books in the world.

When you read a work of literature in an English class, however, you're being asked to read in a special way: you're being asked to perform *literary analysis*. To analyze something means to break it down into smaller parts and then examine how those parts work, both individually and together. Literary analysis involves examining all the parts of a novel, play, short story, or poem—elements such as character, setting, tone, and imagery—and thinking about how the author uses those elements to create certain effects.

A literary essay isn't a book review: you're not being asked whether or not you liked a book or whether you'd recommend it to another reader. A literary essay also isn't like the kind of book report you wrote when you were younger, where your teacher wanted you to summarize the book's action. A high school- or college-level literary essay asks, "How does this piece of literature actually work?" "How does it do what it does?" and, "Why might the author have made the choices he or she did?"

The Seven Steps
No one is born knowing how to analyze literature; it's a skill you learn and a process you can master. As you gain more practice with this kind of thinking and writing, you'll be able to craft a method that works best for you. But until then, here are seven basic steps to writing a well-constructed literary essay:

1. *Ask questions*
2. *Collect evidence*
3. *Construct a thesis*

65

4. Develop and organize arguments
5. Write the introduction
6. Write the body paragraphs
7. Write the conclusion

1. ASK QUESTIONS

When you're assigned a literary essay in class, your teacher will often provide you with a list of writing prompts. Lucky you! Now all you have to do is choose one. Do yourself a favor and pick a topic that interests you. You'll have a much better (not to mention easier) time if you start off with something you enjoy thinking about. If you are asked to come up with a topic by yourself, though, you might start to feel a little panicked. Maybe you have too many ideas—or none at all. Don't worry. Take a deep breath and start by asking yourself these questions:

- **What struck you?** Did a particular image, line, or scene linger in your mind for a long time? If it fascinated you, chances are you can draw on it to write a fascinating essay.

- **What confused you?** Maybe you were surprised to see a character act in a certain way, or maybe you didn't understand why the book ended the way it did. Confusing moments in a work of literature are like a loose thread in a sweater: if you pull on it, you can unravel the entire thing. Ask yourself why the author chose to write about that character or scene the way he or she did and you might tap into some important insights about the work as a whole.

- **Did you notice any patterns?** Is there a phrase that the main character uses constantly or an image that repeats throughout the book? If you can figure out how that pattern weaves through the work and what the significance of that pattern is, you've almost got your entire essay mapped out.

- **Did you notice any contradictions or ironies?** Great works of literature are complex; great literary essays recognize and explain those complexities. Maybe the title (*Happy Days*) totally disagrees with the book's subject matter (hungry orphans dying in the woods). Maybe the main character acts one way around his family and a completely different way around his friends and associates. If you can find a way to explain a work's contradictory elements, you've got the seeds of a great essay.

At this point, you don't need to know exactly what you're going to say about your topic; you just need a place to begin your exploration. You can help direct your reading and brainstorming by formulating your topic as a *question,* which you'll then try to answer in your essay. The best questions invite critical debates and discussions, not just a rehashing of the summary. Remember, you're looking for something you can *prove or argue* based on evidence you find in the text. Finally, remember to keep the scope of your question in mind: is this a topic you can adequately address within the word or page limit you've been given? Conversely, is this a topic big enough to fill the required length?

GOOD QUESTIONS

"Are Romeo and Juliet's parents responsible for the deaths of their children?"

"Why do pigs keep showing up in LORD OF THE FLIES?"

"Are Dr. Frankenstein and his monster alike? How?"

BAD QUESTIONS

"What happens to Scout in TO KILL A MOCKINGBIRD?"

"What do the other characters in JULIUS CAESAR *think about Caesar?"*

"How does Hester Prynne in THE SCARLET LETTER *remind me of my sister?"*

---

2. COLLECT EVIDENCE

Once you know what question you want to answer, it's time to scour the book for things that will help you answer the question. Don't worry if you don't know what you want to say yet—right now you're just collecting ideas and material and letting it all percolate. Keep track of passages, symbols, images, or scenes that deal with your topic. Eventually, you'll start making connections between these examples and your thesis will emerge.

Here's a brief summary of the various parts that compose each and every work of literature. These are the elements that you will analyze in your essay, and which you will offer as evidence to support your arguments. For more on the parts of literary works, see the Glossary of Literary Terms at the end of this section.

LITERARY ANALYSIS

ELEMENTS OF STORY   These are the *what*s of the work—what happens, where it happens, and to whom it happens.

- **Plot:** All of the events and actions of the work.

- **Character:** The people who act and are acted upon in a literary work. The main character of a work is known as the *protagonist.*

- **Conflict:** The central tension in the work. In most cases, the protagonist wants something, while opposing forces (antagonists) hinder the protagonist's progress.

- **Setting:** When and where the work takes place. Elements of setting include location, time period, time of day, weather, social atmosphere, and economic conditions.

- **Narrator:** The person telling the story. The narrator may straightforwardly report what happens, convey the subjective opinions and perceptions of one or more characters, or provide commentary and opinion in his or her own voice.

- **Themes:** The main idea or message of the work—usually an abstract idea about people, society, or life in general. A work may have many themes, which may be in tension with one another.

ELEMENTS OF STYLE   These are the *how*s—how the characters speak, how the story is constructed, and how language is used throughout the work.

- **Structure and organization:** How the parts of the work are assembled. Some novels are narrated in a linear, chronological fashion, while others skip around in time. Some plays follow a traditional three- or five-act structure, while others are a series of loosely connected scenes. Some authors deliberately leave gaps in their works, leaving readers to puzzle out the missing information. A work's structure and organization can tell you a lot about the kind of message it wants to convey.

- **Point of view:** The perspective from which a story is told. In *first-person point of view,* the narrator involves him or herself in the story. ("I went to the store"; "We watched in horror as the bird slammed into the window.") A first-person narrator is usually the protagonist of the work, but not always. In *third-person point of view,* the narrator does not participate in the story. A third-person narrator may closely follow a specific character, recounting that individual character's thoughts or experiences, or it may be what we call an *omniscient* narrator. Omniscient narrators see and know all: they can witness any event in any time or place and are privy to the inner thoughts and feelings of all characters. Remember that the narrator and the author are not the same thing!

- **Diction:** Word choice. Whether a character uses dry, clinical language or flowery prose with lots of exclamation points can tell you a lot about his or her attitude and personality.

- **Syntax:** Word order and sentence construction. Syntax is a crucial part of establishing an author's narrative voice. Ernest Hemingway, for example, is known for writing in very short, straightforward sentences, while James Joyce characteristically wrote in long, incredibly complicated lines.

- **Tone:** The mood or feeling of the text. Diction and syntax often contribute to the tone of a work. A novel written in short, clipped sentences that use small, simple words might feel brusque, cold, or matter-of-fact.

- **Imagery:** Language that appeals to the senses, representing things that can be seen, smelled, heard, tasted, or touched.

- **Figurative language:** Language that is not meant to be interpreted literally. The most common types of figurative language are *metaphors* and *similes,* which compare two unlike things in order to suggest a similarity between them— for example, "All the world's a stage," or "The moon is like a ball of green cheese." (Metaphors say one thing *is* another thing; similes claim that one thing is *like* another thing.)

---

3. CONSTRUCT A THESIS

When you've examined all the evidence you've collected and know how you want to answer the question, it's time to write your thesis statement. A *thesis* is a claim about a work of literature that needs to be supported by evidence and arguments. The thesis statement is the heart of the literary essay, and the bulk of your paper will be spent trying to prove this claim. A good thesis will be:

- **Arguable**. "*The Great Gatsby* describes New York society in the 1920s" isn't a thesis—it's a fact.

- **Provable through textual evidence.** "*Hamlet* is a confusing but ultimately very well-written play" is a weak thesis because it offers the writer's personal opinion about the book. Yes, it's arguable, but it's not a claim that can be proved or supported with examples taken from the play itself.

- **Surprising.** "Both George and Lenny change a great deal in *Of Mice and Men*" is a weak thesis because it's obvious. A really strong thesis will argue for a reading of the text that is not immediately apparent.

- **Specific.** "Dr. Frankenstein's monster tells us a lot about the human condition" is *almost* a really great thesis statement, but it's still too vague. What does the writer mean by "a lot"? *How* does the monster tell us so much about the human condition?

GOOD THESIS STATEMENTS

Question: In *Romeo and Juliet*, which is more powerful in shaping the lovers' story: fate or foolishness?

Thesis: "Though Shakespeare defines Romeo and Juliet as 'star-crossed lovers' and images of stars and planets appear throughout the play, a closer examination of that celestial imagery reveals that the stars are merely witnesses to the characters' foolish activities and not the causes themselves."

Question: How does the bell jar function as a symbol in Sylvia Plath's *The Bell Jar*?

Thesis: "A bell jar is a bell-shaped glass that has three basic uses: to hold a specimen for observation, to contain gases, and to maintain a vacuum. The bell jar appears in each of these capacities in *The Bell Jar*, Plath's semi-autobiographical novel, and each appearances marks a different stage in Esther's mental breakdown."

Question: Would Piggy in *The Lord of the Flies* make a good island leader if he were given the chance?

Thesis: "Though the intelligent, rational, and innovative Piggy has the mental characteristics of a good leader, he ultimately lacks the social skills necessary to be an effective one. Golding emphasizes this point by giving Piggy a foil in the charismatic Jack, whose magnetic personality allows him to capture and wield power effectively, if not always wisely."

4. DEVELOP AND ORGANIZE ARGUMENTS

The reasons and examples that support your thesis will form the middle paragraphs of your essay. Since you can't really write your thesis statement until you know how you'll structure your argument, you'll probably end up working on steps 3 and 4 at the same time.

There's no single method of argumentation that will work in every context. One essay prompt might ask you to compare and contrast two characters, while another asks you to trace an image through a given work of literature. These questions require different kinds of answers and therefore different kinds of arguments. Below, we'll discuss three common kinds of essay prompts and some strategies for constructing a solid, well-argued case.

TYPES OF LITERARY ESSAYS

- **Compare and contrast**

  Compare and contrast the characters of Huck and Jim in THE ADVENTURES OF HUCKLEBERRY FINN.

  Chances are you've written this kind of essay before. In an academic literary context, you'll organize your arguments the same way you would in any other class. You can either go *subject by subject* or *point by point*. In the former, you'll discuss one character first and then the second. In the latter, you'll choose several traits (attitude toward life, social status, images and metaphors associated with the character) and devote a paragraph to each. You may want to use a mix of these two approaches—for example, you may want to spend a paragraph a piece broadly sketching Huck's and Jim's personalities before transitioning into a paragraph or two that describes a few key points of comparison. This can be a highly effective strategy if you want to make a counterintuitive argument—that, despite seeming to be totally different, the two objects being compared are actually similar in a very important way (or vice versa). Remember that your essay should reveal something fresh or unexpected about the text, so think beyond the obvious parallels and differences.

- **Trace**

  Choose an image—for example, birds, knives, or eyes—and trace that image throughout MACBETH.

  Sounds pretty easy, right? All you need to do is read the play, underline every appearance of a knife in *Macbeth,* and then list them in your essay in the order they appear, right? Well, not exactly. Your teacher doesn't want a simple catalog of examples. He or she wants to see you make *connections* between those examples—that's the difference between summarizing and analyzing. In the *Macbeth* example above, think about the different contexts in which knives appear in the play and to what effect. In *Macbeth,* there are real knives and imagined knives; knives that kill and knives that simply threaten. Categorize and classify your examples to give them some order. Finally, always keep the overall effect in mind. After you choose and analyze your examples, you should come to some greater understanding about the work, as well as your chosen image, symbol, or phrase's role in developing the major themes and stylistic strategies of that work.

- **Debate**

    Is the society depicted in 1984 *good for its citizens?*

    In this kind of essay, you're being asked to debate a moral, ethical, or aesthetic issue regarding the work. You might be asked to judge a character or group of characters (*Is Caesar responsible for his own demise?*) or the work itself (*Is* JANE EYRE *a feminist novel?*). For this kind of essay, there are two important points to keep in mind. First, don't simply base your arguments on your personal feelings and reactions. Every literary essay expects you to read and analyze the work, so search for evidence in the text. What do characters in *1984* have to say about the government of Oceania? What images does Orwell use that might give you a hint about his attitude toward the government? As in any debate, you also need to make sure that you define all the necessary terms before you begin to argue your case. What does it mean to be a "good" society? What makes a novel "feminist"? You should define your terms right up front, in the first paragraph after your introduction.

    Second, remember that strong literary essays make contrary and surprising arguments. Try to think outside the box. In the *1984* example above, it seems like the obvious answer would be no, the totalitarian society depicted in Orwell's novel is *not* good for its citizens. But can you think of any arguments for the opposite side? Even if your final assertion is that the novel depicts a cruel, repressive, and therefore harmful society, acknowledging and responding to the counterargument will strengthen your overall case.

5. WRITE THE INTRODUCTION

Your introduction sets up the entire essay. It's where you present your topic and articulate the particular issues and questions you'll be addressing. It's also where you, as the writer, introduce yourself to your readers. A persuasive literary essay immediately establishes its writer as a knowledgeable, authoritative figure.

An introduction can vary in length depending on the over-all length of the essay, but in a traditional five-paragraph essay it should be no longer than one paragraph. However long it is, your introduction needs to:

- **Provide any necessary context.** Your introduction should situate the reader and let him or her know what to expect. What book are you discussing? Which characters? What topic will you be addressing?

- **Answer the "So what?" question.** Why is this topic important, and why is your particular position on the topic noteworthy? Ideally, your introduction should pique the reader's interest by suggesting how your argument is surprising or otherwise counterintuitive. Literary essays make unexpected connections and reveal less-than-obvious truths.

- **Present your thesis.** This usually happens at or very near the end of your introduction.

- **Indicate the shape of the essay to come.** Your reader should finish reading your introduction with a good sense of the scope of your essay as well as the path you'll take toward proving your thesis. You don't need to spell out every step, but you do need to suggest the organizational pattern you'll be using.

Your introduction should not:

- **Be vague.** Beware of the two killer words in literary analysis: *interesting* and *important*. Of course the work, question, or example is interesting and important—that's why you're writing about it!

- **Open with any grandiose assertions.** Many student readers think that beginning their essays with a flamboyant statement such as, "Since the dawn of time, writers have been fascinated with the topic of free will," makes them sound important and commanding. You know what? It actually sounds pretty amateurish.

- **Wildly praise the work.** Another typical mistake student writers make is extolling the work or author. Your teacher doesn't need to be told that "Shakespeare is perhaps the greatest writer in the English language." You can mention a work's reputation in passing—by referring to *The Adventures of Huckleberry Finn* as "Mark Twain's enduring classic," for example—but don't make a point of bringing it up unless that reputation is key to your argument.

- **Go off-topic.** Keep your introduction streamlined and to the point. Don't feel the need to throw in all kinds of bells and whistles in order to impress your reader—just get to the point as quickly as you can, without skimping on any of the required steps.

---

6. WRITE THE BODY PARAGRAPHS

Once you've written your introduction, you'll take the arguments you developed in step 4 and turn them into your body paragraphs. The organization of this middle section of your essay will largely be determined by the argumentative strategy you use, but no matter how you arrange your thoughts, your body paragraphs need to do the following:

- **Begin with a strong topic sentence.** Topic sentences are like signs on a highway: they tell the reader where they are and where they're going. A good topic sentence not only alerts readers to what issue will be discussed in the following paragraph but also gives them a sense of what argument will be made *about* that issue. "Rumor and gossip play an important role in *The Crucible*" isn't a strong topic sentence because it doesn't tell us very much. "The community's constant gossiping creates an environment that allows false accusations to flourish" is a much stronger topic sentence— it not only tells us *what* the paragraph will discuss (gossip) but *how* the paragraph will discuss the topic (by showing how gossip creates a set of conditions that leads to the play's climactic action).

- **Fully and completely develop a single thought.** Don't skip around in your paragraph or try to stuff in too much material. Body paragraphs are like bricks: each individual one needs to be strong and sturdy or the entire structure will collapse. Make sure you have really proven your point before moving on to the next one.

- **Use transitions effectively.** Good literary essay writers know that each paragraph must be clearly and strongly linked to the material around it. Think of each paragraph as a response to the one that precedes it. Use transition words and phrases such as *however, similarly, on the contrary, therefore,* and *furthermore* to indicate what kind of response you're making.

---

7. WRITE THE CONCLUSION

Just as you used the introduction to ground your readers in the topic before providing your thesis, you'll use the conclusion to quickly summarize the specifics learned thus far and then hint at the broader implications of your topic. A good conclusion will:

- **Do more than simply restate the thesis.** If your thesis argued that *The Catcher in the Rye* can be read as a Christian allegory, don't simply end your essay by saying, "And that is why *The Catcher in the Rye* can be read as a Christian allegory." If you've constructed your arguments well, this kind of statement will just be redundant.

- **Synthesize the arguments, not summarize them.** Similarly, don't repeat the details of your body paragraphs in your conclusion. The reader has already read your essay, and chances are it's not so long that they've forgotten all your points by now.

- **Revisit the "So what?" question.** In your introduction, you made a case for why your topic and position are important. You should close your essay with the same sort of gesture. What do your readers know now that they didn't know before? How will that knowledge help them better appreciate or understand the work overall?

- **Move from the specific to the general.** Your essay has most likely treated a very specific element of the work—a single character, a small set of images, or a particular passage. In your conclusion, try to show how this narrow discussion has wider implications for the work overall. If your essay on *To Kill a Mockingbird* focused on the character of Boo Radley, for example, you might want to include a bit in your conclusion about how he fits into the novel's larger message about childhood, innocence, or family life.

- **Stay relevant.** Your conclusion should suggest new directions of thought, but it shouldn't be treated as an opportunity to pad your essay with all the extra, interesting ideas you came up with during your brainstorming sessions but couldn't fit into the essay proper. Don't attempt to stuff in unrelated queries or too many abstract thoughts.

- **Avoid making overblown closing statements.** A conclusion should open up your highly specific, focused discussion, but it should do so without drawing a sweeping lesson about life or human nature. Making such observations may be part of the point of reading, but it's almost always a mistake in essays, where these observations tend to sound overly dramatic or simply silly.

A+ Essay Checklist

Congratulations! If you've followed all the steps we've outlined above, you should have a solid literary essay to show for all your efforts. What if you've got your sights set on an A+? To write the kind of superlative essay that will be rewarded with a perfect grade, keep the following rubric in mind. These are the qualities that teachers expect to see in a truly A+ essay. How does yours stack up?

- ✓ Demonstrates a thorough understanding of the book
- ✓ Presents an original, compelling argument
- ✓ Thoughtfully analyzes the text's formal elements
- ✓ Uses appropriate and insightful examples
- ✓ Structures ideas in a logical and progressive order
- ✓ Demonstrates a mastery of sentence construction, transitions, grammar, spelling, and word choice

SUGGESTED ESSAY TOPICS

1. *Though* JULIUS CAESAR *focuses on the struggles between powerful men, what role do the plebeians, or common people, play? Are they as fickle as Flavius and Murellus claim in the opening scene? How important is their support to the successes of the various military leaders and the outcome of the play? The play depicts Rome at a time of transition between republic and empire—a time in which, theoretically, the Roman people are losing their power. What role do the people themselves play in this transition?*

2. *Consider Brutus's actions. Is he right to join the conspiracy against Caesar? What are his reasons? Does he choose to join the conspiracy, or is he tricked by Cassius? How do Cassius's motivations compare to Brutus's? Are they more noble or less noble?*

3. JULIUS CAESAR, *a play about statehood and leadership, is one of the most quoted of Shakespeare's plays in modern-day political speeches. Why do you think this play about conspiracy and assassination might appeal to politicians today? Also, discuss how this play might have been a reflection on Elizabethan politics, keeping in mind that Queen Elizabeth, like Caesar, was an aging, heirless leader.*

4. *Discuss friendship in the play. Consider Caesar and Brutus, Caesar and Antony, Brutus and Cassius, Antony and Octavius, or any other pairings. Are these true friendships or merely political alliances forged for the sake of convenience and self-preservation? How do they compare with the heterosexual relationships in the play—the relations between husbands and wives? Are they more profound or less profound, more revealing or less revealing of their participants' characters?*

5. *Who is the protagonist in this play? Is it Caesar, who dies well before the end but whose power and name continue on? Or is it Brutus, the noble man who falls because of his tragic flaws?*

6.   Consider theatricality in this play. Think particularly of
     the scene of Caesar's murder (and Cassius's reference to
     future productions of the scene), the speeches in the Forum
     (particularly Antony's), and the speeches given over the dead
     conspirators. How do acting and rhetoric affect the events of
     the play? How do they interact with politics? Does the play
     reference its own political power as a theatrical production?

7.   Discuss inflexibility in this play, focusing on Caesar and
     Brutus. How is each man inflexible? Is this rigidity an
     admirable trait or a flaw? Do the rewards of this rigidity
     outweigh the consequences, or vice versa?

A+ Student Essay

How are woman portrayed in *Julius Caesar*?

Julius Caesar is a play about men: their relationships, their culture, and their actions. In the male-dominated world of ancient Rome, characters have a distinct understanding of what it means to be or act like a man. Women in *Julius Caesar* represent everything that Roman men are not supposed to be—however, the utter disdain men show for feminine traits eventually proves shortsighted, as the play argues that women and their special gifts are not to be taken lightly.

In *Julius Caesar,* masculinity implies not only bravery, but also steadfastness. The opposite traits—weakness, fearfulness, and inconstancy—are mainly associated with women. Male characters continuously use terms such as "womanish" to taunt other men perceived as timid or tractable. Brutus refers to the "melting spirits of women" (2.1.121), and Caesar's call for water following his epileptic seizure is derided as the actions of " a sick girl" (1.2.130). When men do exhibit signs of wavering, they often blame their temporary weakness on their mothers, whose "spirits" counteract the decisive, stalwart natures they have inherited from their fathers. At one point, Casca describes "three or four wenches" enthusiastically forgiving Caesar for his fit and claims that they would have done the same if Caesar had stabbed their own mothers, furthering the portrait of women as fickle, foolish, and gullible (1.2.267–269).

The female characters of *Julius Caesar* seem to internalize these distinctions as well. Portia makes several blanket statements about the female character, exclaiming, "How hard it is for women to keep counsel!" and "How weak a thing / The heart of woman is!" (2.4.8; 2.4.41–42). Fearing for her husband's safety, she contrasts her firm, resolute "man's heart," which can withstand the strain, with her timorous "woman's might" (2.4.7). Just as the men perceive the influence of their mothers and fathers as being at odds within their own selves, Portia sees a masculine side of herself competing with her feminine nature.

Similarly, when Portia wishes to claim power for herself, she does so by invoking her male ancestors, inverting the male tendency to blame their undesirable qualities on their female ancestors. After Brutus refuses to acknowledge that her status as wife earns her the right to share his secrets, she takes a contrary tack and tries to appeal to him as a kind of fellow male. She claims that being descended from the great Cato, not to mention having been chosen by Brutus himself, makes her "stronger than [her] sex, / Being so fathered and so husbanded" (2.1.295–296). Then, to further prove her emotional and physical strength, she stabs herself in the thigh. Throughout the play, men swear that they are not afraid to face death or injury; Portia proves her manliness by making good on those boasts.

However, the play does present women as sharing a powerful, characteristically feminine trait: They each exhibit an instinctive type of foresight. The men of *Julius Caesar*, though powerful, are often caught unawares by their fate. Caesar refuses to heed the warnings of his own death, just as Brutus misguidedly believes the people will applaud Caesar's assassination. The play seems to suggest that the same resoluteness the Romans revere as a supreme masculine virtue can become a liability when it turns into inflexibility and imperceptiveness. Calphurnia and Portia both anticipate the dangers ahead. Like animals that sense the arrival of an earthquake, the women seem tuned to a different frequency. Calphurnia dreams of Caesar's statue pouring forth blood, with smiling Romans washing their hands in the flow. Decius scoffs at her fear, but Calphurnia knows that her dream portends ill luck for Caesar. Like an oracle, the unconscious Calphurnia predicts the future, and her three cries of "Help, ho! They murder Caesar!" has the force of prophecy (2.2.3). Similarly, long before Brutus's downfall, Portia claims to have heard a tumultuous clamor on "the wind . . . from the Capitol," which she interprets as trouble for her husband (2.4.20). Later, when she senses the sea change about to take place, she kills herself preemptively. Her suicide, described in mythical, grotesque terms, serves as yet another portent Brutus ignores.

It would be too much to say that *Julius Caesar* valorizes women, but it does associate them with supernatural prescience. Certainly the play suggests that, if their advice had been followed, their husbands might have avoided some of the calamities that befall them. But in the end, the female characters in *Julius Caesar* become collateral damage in the tragedy, unable to escape what they foresee.

GLOSSARY OF LITERARY TERMS

ANTAGONIST
> The entity that acts to frustrate the goals of the *protagonist*. The antagonist is usually another *character* but may also be a non-human force.

ANTIHERO / ANTIHEROINE
> A *protagonist* who is not admirable or who challenges notions of what should be considered admirable.

CHARACTER
> A person, animal, or any other thing with a personality that appears in a *narrative*.

CLIMAX
> The moment of greatest intensity in a text or the major turning point in the *plot*.

CONFLICT
> The central struggle that moves the *plot* forward. The conflict can be the *protagonist*'s struggle against fate, nature, society, or another person.

FIRST-PERSON POINT OF VIEW
> A literary style in which the *narrator* tells the story from his or her own *point of view* and refers to himself or herself as "I." The narrator may be an active participant in the story or just an observer.

HERO / HEROINE
> The principal *character* in a literary work or *narrative*.

IMAGERY
> Language that brings to mind sense-impressions, representing things that can be seen, smelled, heard, tasted, or touched.

MOTIF
> A recurring idea, structure, contrast, or device that develops or informs the major *themes* of a work of literature.

NARRATIVE
> A story.

LITERARY ANALYSIS

NARRATOR

The person (sometimes a *character*) who tells a story; the *voice* assumed by the writer. The narrator and the author of the work of literature are not the same person.

PLOT

The arrangement of the events in a story, including the sequence in which they are told, the relative emphasis they are given, and the causal connections between events.

POINT OF VIEW

The *perspective* that a *narrative* takes toward the events it describes.

PROTAGONIST

The main *character* around whom the story revolves.

SETTING

The location of a *narrative* in time and space. Setting creates mood or atmosphere.

SUBPLOT

A secondary *plot* that is of less importance to the overall story but may serve as a point of contrast or comparison to the main plot.

SYMBOL

An object, *character,* figure, or color that is used to represent an abstract idea or concept. Unlike an *emblem,* a symbol may have different meanings in different contexts.

SYNTAX

The way the words in a piece of writing are put together to form lines, phrases, or clauses; the basic structure of a piece of writing.

THEME

A fundamental and universal idea explored in a literary work.

TONE

The author's attitude toward the subject or *characters* of a story or poem or toward the reader.

VOICE

An author's individual way of using language to reflect his or her own personality and attitudes. An author communicates voice through *tone, diction,* and *syntax.*

A Note on Plagiarism

Plagiarism—presenting someone else's work as your own—rears its ugly head in many forms. Many students know that copying text without citing it is unacceptable. But some don't realize that even if you're not quoting directly, but instead are paraphrasing or summarizing, *it is plagiarism* unless you cite the source.

Here are the most common forms of plagiarism:

- Using an author's phrases, sentences, or paragraphs without citing the source
- Paraphrasing an author's ideas without citing the source
- Passing off another student's work as your own

How do you steer clear of plagiarism? You should *always* acknowledge all words and ideas that aren't your own by using quotation marks around verbatim text or citations like footnotes and endnotes to note another writer's ideas. For more information on how to give credit when credit is due, ask your teacher for guidance or visit www.sparknotes.com.

REVIEW & RESOURCES

QUIZ

1. How does Caesar first enter the play?

   A. In disgrace; he has been captured
   B. In defeat
   C. In a triumphal procession; he has defeated the sons of his deceased rival, Pompey
   D. In disguise

2. What does the Soothsayer say to Caesar?

   A. "Beware the Ides of March"
   B. "Never trust Cassius"
   C. "Pursue the kingship"
   D. "Your toupee is on backward"

3. What does Cassius first ask Brutus?

   A. What happened at the battle
   B. Where his wife is
   C. Why he has been so distant and contemplative lately
   D. Whether he wants to be king instead of Caesar

4. What does Brutus admit to Cassius?

   A. That his wife is dead
   B. That he and Antony have had an argument
   C. That he thinks the Senate is doomed
   D. That he fears the people want Caesar to be king

5. What does Antony offer Caesar in the marketplace?

   A. The crown
   B. The key to the city
   C. A newspaper
   D. A new chariot

6.   That night, which of the following omens are seen?

   A.   Dead men walking
   B.   Lions strolling in the marketplace
   C.   Lightning
   D.   All of the above

7.   What finally convinces Brutus to join the conspirators?

   A.   Forged letters planted by Cassius
   B.   Visits from the citizens
   C.   His intuition
   D.   Omens

8.   Why does Calpurnia urge Caesar to stay home rather than appear at the Senate?

   A.   He travels too much; they have hardly seen each other lately.
   B.   His grandchildren are coming to visit.
   C.   He does not appear presentable enough.
   D.   She has had nightmares about his death.

9.   Why does Caesar ignore Calpurnia's warnings?

   A.   He is deaf in one ear and fails to hear her correctly.
   B.   Decius convinces him that Calpurnia has interpreted the dream and the omens incorrectly.
   C.   He wants fresh air.
   D.   He wants to humor the conspirators.

10.   What does Artemidorus offer Caesar in the street?

   A.   A letter warning him about the conspiracy
   B.   A victory wreath
   C.   A new shield
   D.   The crown

11.   What do the conspirators do at the Senate?

   A.   Kneel around Caesar
   B.   Stab him to death
   C.   Proclaim "Tyranny is dead!"
   D.   All of the above

12. What does Antony do when he arrives at Caesar's body?

    A. He swears allegiance to Brutus.
    B. He weeps over Caesar's body.
    C. He shakes hands with the conspirators.
    D. All of the above

13. After the assassination of Caesar, which of the conspirators addresses the plebeians first?

    A. Decius
    B. Cassius
    C. Antony
    D. Brutus

14. What is Brutus's explanation for killing Caesar?

    A. Caesar was ambitious.
    B. Caesar was old.
    C. Caesar was evil.
    D. Caesar was weak.

15. What does Antony tell the crowd?

    A. That Brutus is an honorable man
    B. That Caesar brought riches to Rome and turned down the crown
    C. That Caesar bequeathed all of the citizens a large sum of money
    D. All of the above

16. What is the crowd's response?

    A. Apathy; they did not care for Caesar and his ambition
    B. Indifference; Antony's rhetoric does not move them
    C. Rage; they chase the conspirators from the city
    D. Irritation; they are tired of Antony's constant complaints

17. Who is Octavius?

  A. Antony's cousin
  B. Brutus's son
  C. Caesar's adopted son and appointed heir
  D. Cassius's best friend

18. Octavius and Antony join together with whom?

  A. Titinius
  B. Casca
  C. Cinna
  D. Lepidus

19. Why do Brutus and Cassius argue?

  A. They are tired of each other's company.
  B. Cassius seduced Brutus's wife.
  C. Brutus asked for money and Cassius withheld it.
  D. They disagree on the best tactics for the upcoming battle.

20. What news do Brutus and Cassius receive from Rome?

  A. Portia is dead.
  B. Many senators are dead.
  C. The armies of Antony and Octavius are marching toward Philippi.
  D. All of the above

21. What appears at Brutus's bedside in camp?

  A. A crow
  B. Caesar's ghost
  C. A bloody dagger
  D. A lion

22. What does Cassius think has happened to his and Brutus's armies?

    A. He believes that they have been defeated by Antony and Octavius.

    B. He thinks that they have won.

    C. He believes that they have joined the ranks of Antony and Octavius.

    D. He thinks that they have been felled by an epidemic.

23. What is Cassius's response to the situation?

    A. He gives himself up to Antony and Octavius.

    B. He flees.

    C. He waits quietly for it all to end.

    D. He has his servant stab him.

24. What does Brutus do when he sees the battle lost?

    A. He joins Antony's side.

    B. He kills himself.

    C. He gives himself up as a prisoner to Antony and Octavius.

    D. He flees.

25. What does Antony call Brutus?

    A. A scoundrel

    B. A bad soldier

    C. A coward

    D. The noblest Roman

ANSWER KEY

1: C; 2: A; 3: C; 4: D; 5: A; 6: D; 7: A; 8: D; 9: B; 10: A; 11: D; 12: D; 13: D; 14: A; 15: D; 16: C; 17: C; 18: D; 19: D; 20: D; 21: B; 22: A; 23: D; 24: B; 25: D

Suggestions for Further Reading

BLOOM, HAROLD, ed. JULIUS CAESAR: *Modern Critical Interpretations*. New York: Chelsea House Publishers, 1992.

DANIELL, DAVID, ed. JULIUS CAESAR: *The Arden Shakespeare*. New York: Wadsworth Publishing Co., 1998.

EISAMAN MAUS, KATHERINE. "JULIUS CAESAR." In *The Norton Shakespeare*. Edited by Stephen Greenblatt. New York: W. W. Norton & Co., 1997.

NARDO, DON. *The Importance of* JULIUS CAESAR. San Diego: Lucent Books, 1996.

———, ed. *Readings on* JULIUS CAESAR. San Diego: Greenhaven Press, 1998.

SHAKESPEARE, WILLIAM. *The Tragedy of Julius Caesar*. New Folger Library Edition. Edited by Barbara A. Mowat and Paul Werstine. New York: Washington Square Press, 1992.

———. THE TRAGEDY OF JULIUS CAESAR: *With New and Updated Critical Essays and a Revised Bibliography*. Signet Classics Edition. Edited by William and Barbara Rosen. New York: Penguin Books, Inc., 1998.

REVIEW & RESOURCES